Water Bath Canning for Beginners and Beyond

The Essential Guide to Safe Water Bath Canning at Home. Easy and Delicious Recipes for Jams, Jellies, Salsas, Pickled Vegetables, and More!

By
Linda C. Johnson

© Copyright 2022 - All rights reserved.

The content contained within this book may not be reproduced, duplicated or transmitted without direct written permission from the author or the publisher.

Under no circumstances will any blame or legal responsibility be held against the publisher, or author, for any damages, reparation, or monetary loss due to the information contained within this book, either directly or indirectly.

Legal Notice:

This book is copyright protected. It is only for personal use. You cannot amend, distribute, sell, use, quote or paraphrase any part, or the content within this book, without the consent of the author or publisher.

Disclaimer Notice:

Please note the information contained within this document is for educational and entertainment purposes only. All effort has been executed to present accurate, up to date, reliable, complete information. No warranties of any kind are declared or implied. Readers acknowledge that the author is not engaged in the rendering of legal, financial, medical or professional advice. The content within this book has been derived from various sources. Please consult a licensed professional before attempting any techniques outlined in this book.

By reading this document, the reader agrees that under no circumstances is the author responsible for any losses, direct or indirect, that are incurred as a result of the use of the information contained within this document, including, but not limited to, errors, omissions, or inaccuracies.

Table of Contents

Introduction 13

Chapter 1 Water Bath Canning 101 18

    What is Water Bath Canning? 18

    When to Use a Water Bath Canner.. 20

    Water Bath Canning Equipment 22

    Choosing a Canning Recipe 24

    Other Helpful Tips 26

    Key Chapter 1 Takeaways 28

Chapter 2 How to Water Bath Can in 4 Easy Steps 30

    Step 1: Preparation 30

    Step 2: Heating 32

    Step 3: Cooling 35

    Step 4: Storing 37

    Key Chapter 2 Takeaways..38

Chapter 3 Jams, Marmalades, Chutneys, and Jellies...................................... 40

    Jam Recipes 40

    Marmalade Recipes 45

    Chutney Recipes 52

    It Takes Two to Mango Chutney...52

- Jelly Recipes 57
- Key Chapter 3 Takeaways 62

Chapter 4 Desserts 64
- Canning Desserts 101 64
- Fruit Recipes 66
  - Blasting Blueberries 66
  - Rockin Raspberries 67
  - Krazy Kiwi 69
- Pie Filling Recipes 70
  - Granny's Apple Pie Filling 70
  - The Great Rhubarb Pie Filling 72
  - Cherry Bomb Pie Filling 74
- Fruit Sauce Recipes 76
  - Lemon Zest Blueberry Sauce 76
  - Awesomesauce Applesauce 78
  - Cinnamon Pear Sauce 79
- Key Chapter 4 Takeaways 81

Chapter 5 Pickles 83
- Pickling 101 83
- Pickled Vegetables 85

  Dill With It Pickles 85

  In a Real Pickle Pickled Onions 87

  Rise and Brine Pickled Vegetable Mix 89

 Pickled Fruit 91

  Perfect Pickled Peaches 91

  Picturesque Pickled Apricots 93

  Popular Pickled Fruit Cocktail 95

 Relish 97

  Relished Dill Pickled Relish 97

  Relished Sweet Pickled Relish 99

  Relished Jalapeno Relish 100

 Key Chapter 5 Takeaways 102

Chapter 6 Tomatoes 104

 Tomato Recipes 104

  Dice to Meet You Diced Tomatoes 104

  Cherished Cherry Tomatoes 106

  Whole Lotta Whole Tomato 108

 Salsa Recipes 109

  Mild Salsa 110

  Spicy Salsa 111

Salsa Verde 113

Tomato Sauce Recipes 116

Pasta La Vista, Baby Sauce..116

Marinara Sauce.. 118

Pizza Sauce 120

Tomato Juice Recipes 122

Tomato Juice 122

Fresh From the Garden Vegetable Juice................................. 124

Bloody Mary 126

Chapter 7 Condiments..130

Basic Condiments 130

Knock 'Em Out Ketchup..130

Better Barbecue Sauce... 132

Marry Me Mustard 134

Advanced Condiments 136

Serenading Sweet Chili Sauce 136

Horseradish Harmony.. 138

From the Heart Honey Mustard 139

Dressing and Syrup Recipes 141

You Won't Regret this Strawberry Vinaigrette 141

      Seriously Good Strawberry Syrup 143

      Best Blueberry Syrup Around 144

  More Sauces 146

      Can't Be Beat Cranberry Sauce 146

      Hot Hot Sauce 148

      The Chicken Wing Sauce 150

  Key Chapter 7 Takeaways 152

Chapter 8: Bonus Chapter - Meals in a Jar 154

  Meal Preparation 154

  What's for Breakfast 156

      Apple Butter on Toast 156

      Greek Yogurt with Mango 158

  What's for Lunch 159

      Peach Salsa Tacos 159

      Cowboy Candy Over Salmon 161

  What's for Dinner 163

      Spaghetti with Zoodles 163

      Pickled Beets Salad 165

  Key Chapter 8 Takeaways 167

Chapter 9 Everything Else you Need to Know 169

- Altitude 169
- Measurement Conversion 172
    - Cooking Temperatures 172
    - Pounds to Kilograms 173
    - EWG's 2021 "Dirty Dozen" 173
    - EWG's 2021 "Clean Fifteen" 174
- Fruit and Tomato Canning Charts 174
- Pesticides 176
- What Can Go Wrong? 176

Conclusion 178

Thank You 181

Glossary 182

Index 185

References 189

Images 194

Your Free Gifts!

Out of all of the available literature on water bath canning, you chose this one. Thank you. As a way to express my gratitude, I'm offering additional valuable resources for FREE to my readers.

Get Free Instant Access by clicking on or going to www.customercore.eu

- **FREE GIFT:** Is My Ultimate 35-Step Cheatsheet For Water Bath Canning Successfully every time.
- **FREE GIFT:** Is My favorite (& secret) Pizza Tomato Sauce Recipe.

While grabbing these gifts, please also enjoy my Pressure Canning resources for **FREE**. These include

- **FREE GIFT:** My Ultimate Checklist For Canning Successfully
- **FREE GIFT:** My 5-Minute Cheat Sheet To Help You Can Safely
- **FREE GIFT:** My 17 Essential Items You Need To Can Successfully

Before we start, I have a small favor to ask of you. When you finish reading this book, **would you please consider posting a review of this book on the platform?** Posting a review will help support my writing. Thank you. I really appreciate it. Just follow the relevant link below.

>> Click Here to leave a review on Amazon US <<

>> Click Here to leave a review on Amazon UK <<

>> Click Here to leave a review on Amazon Canada <<

>> Click Here to leave a review on Amazon Mexico <<

>> Click Here to leave a review on Amazon Brazil <<

>> Click Here to leave a review on Amazon Spain <<

>> Click Here to leave a review on Amazon Italy <<

>> Click Here to leave a review on Amazon France <<

>> Click Here to leave a review on Amazon India <<

Introduction

"Be the change you want to see in the world."

- Gandhi

Every year, over a billion pounds of food is sent to landfills. According to the United States Department of Agriculture (USDA), this is the tragic fate of 30-40% of the entire food supply in the United States (USDA, 2010). This wastes many of the country's resources such as land, water, money, and labor. One of the main contributors to food waste is spoilage. As a consumer, you don't have much power over spoilage that occurs during transit or any other time before the goods reach the market.

This food waste is astronomically bad for both the environment and the economy. With all of this in mind, we should ask ourselves how much food leaves our kitchens in garbage bags.

We owe it to ourselves, our children, and the world around us to try our best as individuals to make a difference. The best place to start is preventing spoilage, and lucky for you this book will tell you exactly how to do that in great detail and deliciousness.

Now you may be thinking, wow, this is really serious stuff. I just picked up this book because I have extra strawberries in my garden and want to save them for a pie I'll make later. Well congratulations, that pie is going to help to save the world. That might be a lot of pressure to put on a pie, but with the delicious recipes offered in this book, you don't have to worry about living up to any expectations. As long as your jar is sealed properly, spoilage will be put off indefinitely; but that isn't the only perk to water bath canning your food. For many canners, the biggest reward to using a water bath canner is the preservation of flavor. What is tastier than a berry out of season? That flavor can only be made better with the knowledge that you're helping eliminate unnecessary food waste.

Saving the world is great, but why else should you start home canning? There are numerous health benefits to this practice. The most important of which is actually knowing every single ingredient that goes into your food. Food companies are only required to list ingredients that make up 5% or more of their product. The only instances where this 5% rule doesn't apply is with additives or allergens. These must be listed no matter how small the percentage is. However, the ingredients that fall under the U.S. Food and Drug Administration (FDA)'s category of major food allergens only account for around 90% of all food allergies. Those who suffer from the other 10% are just kind of out of luck when it comes to buying food. With home canning, you can decide exactly what you put in your jars and you never have to worry about the 4% of mystery ingredients you may be consuming.

Preparing your own meals is also a great way to stay in shape, and home canning is a reliable and more sustainable way to do that. With basic meal preparation techniques, you are preparing your food for a week. This can free up several hours of your week that can then be devoted to family time, or other meaningful activities. With home canning, all you need is a day or two out of the entire *year* and you've got fresh and healthy food whenever you need. When you have a family to feed, you don't always have the time to prepare something. This is when easy and unhealthy options like fast food feel like the only choice. Home canning is the opportunity to prepare a healthy meal for days like these that just can't be scheduled.

Also, eating out is expensive. Buying groceries is expensive. Consuming food because you have to live is expensive. Another way that home canning can make your life easier is by saving you a bit of money. Fresh fruit will only last a couple of days before it starts to rot. If you can't eat it in time, that is as good as throwing your money down the drain. Water bath canning will elongate the life span of your fruit so you don't have to worry about wasting it anymore. Save yourself the frustration of replacing food you've already bought. Having healthy food available will also help during those weeks when payday just isn't coming fast enough. Start canning, and your wallet will thank you.

This all said, water bath canning is not a magical cure-all. The benefits aren't given, they are earned. For example, the equipment isn't hard to use, but it will take some time to get used to the process. It's okay if your first jars don't come out perfectly. It can take several tries before you get the results you want. Don't be afraid to experiment with different ingredient and flavor combinations. The more you put into it, the more you'll get out of it. Think of canning as an investment. With a little bit of time and work, you'll be canning like a professional. So if you want to get healthy, save a little money, and maybe even help the world, then get ready to start your personal canning journey.

Chapter 1
Water Bath Canning 101

"Without a solid foundation, you have trouble creating anything of value."

- **Ericka Oppenheimer**

What is Water Bath Canning?

Water bath canning is an easy method to safely preserve food with high acidic levels. Water bath canning is also referred to as "boiling water canning" or "hot water canning." It is the simple process of boiling jars in a large pot of water for a specified amount of time. Within the pot, the jars are boiled evenly on all sides to ensure the food is thoroughly cooked. After the jars have been boiled and properly sealed, they no longer have to be refrigerated. They will be safely preserved until the jar is opened again as long as they are stored in a cool and dry place.

Produce that is canned in a water bath canner will theoretically last forever. As long as the seal is intact, then the food is still edible. This doesn't mean that the food will be delicious forever, though. After a year, the flavor will start to go downhill and the overall quality will diminish. That's why it's recommended to eat home canned goods within the following 12 months after its processing. I always recommend labeling the jar with the date and having an organized storage system where the oldest products are the easiest to get to and use.

You should also label your jars with the ingredients that you used, and not just what the final product is. Sometimes, it's hard to remember what you put in a jar several months ago, and this way you don't have to rely on your memory. Most of the ingredients used in the recipes in this book will lean more towards healthier options, but that doesn't account for allergens. If you will have to substitute any ingredients, make sure to double-check boiling times as they may differ depending on what you are using. The wrong boiling time could result in under-processed food which will not be safe to eat.

If you choose to substitute an ingredient, it might change whether or not you'll have to raw pack or hot pack. Raw packing is when the food is not cooked before it's packed into the jars. Raw packing is sometimes called cold packing in certain recipes. Hot packing is the opposite, when the food is partially cooked beforehand. After either method, liquid is added to the contents to help preservation. This liquid is usually either boiling water, juice, or syrup. With either method, there should always be around an inch of headspace between the lid and the food or it could seal improperly.

When to Use a Water Bath Canner

Water bath canning isn't the only method of canning. The other method is called pressure canning, and requires a pressure canner that can reach temperatures that the water bath process can't. Also, water bath canners require more water than pressure canners. The food in water bath canning is heated by the boiling water that surrounds it. This means it can only reach the temperature of boiling water, which is 212 °F. Fruits, jams, and pickles are some of the many foods that are safe to process at this temperature. Jars in a pressure canner are heated up by steam that can reach 240 °F. Meat and unpickled vegetables need this higher temperature to process.

So why does some food need higher temperatures to can? It's all about acidity. The acidity of food is measured by its pH level. The pH scale ranges from 0 to 14. Seven is considered neutral since it is in the middle. If something is lower than 7 on the pH scale it is considered acidic. If it is higher, it is considered alkaline. To put this in perspective, lemon juice or vinegar has a pH level of about 2. This makes it acidic and safe to put in a water bath canner. Meat and vegetables are closer to neutral than alkaline but are still considered to be low-acid ranging from 4—7 pH. These levels are used to determine if drinking water has been contaminated or not.

So what will happen if you put low-acid food in a water bath canner? Without exaggerating, you could die. Acidity helps kill dangerous bacteria, but low-acid foods can't do this on their own without reaching certain temperatures. Every canner's biggest fear is catching botulism, the spores of which are mostly found in low-acid foods. So what will happen if you put high-acid food in a pressure canner? It might taste bad. There's not any life-changing risk to it. The worst that could happen is you overcook the food and have to throw it away. (If you're curious about certain foods and their pH levels, you can always contact your local extension service. This is a state agency with the USDA that can provide research and other information.)

Now that you know the difference between the two methods of canning, you may be wondering which one is better in general. Seeing as this is a water bath canning book, we're going to go with that one. In actuality, they are both wonderful methods that have their own pros and cons. Pressure canning is easier to plan meals with while water bath canning is easier to do. Water bath canning is also a cheaper method and a lot less of an investment. You could even call it "no pressure" canning. It is also less dangerous. Modern pressure canners might be incredibly safe but they can still cause a lot of damage if the ventilation becomes clogged. You don't have to worry about your lid possibly flying off into the ceiling if you own a water bath canner.

Water Bath Canning Equipment

You'll never be able to successfully can anything without special canning equipment. While water bath canning is the least expensive option, these purchases are still a must. The first thing you'll need to invest in is a water bath canner. There are specially-made pots for this but all you need is a large pot that can fit jars in it for canning. It's important that the water can cover the jar by 2 inches otherwise the water won't be able to boil. The canner should also have a fitted lid. If you want to go out and buy a special canner then by all means go ahead, it just isn't necessary.

Next you will need a rack to accompany your canner. Racks sit at the bottom of the pot. Their purpose is to make sure the jars aren't touching the bottom of the canner or each other. If jars are put at the bottom of the pot with no rack, the jar's bottom won't heat as evenly as the other sides. If the jars are touching each other they could shake and break, causing glass fragments to go into your food. Water bath canners usually come with racks, but if you're just using a big pot you'll need to make sure the one you buy can fit racks.

You will also need jars to put the food in. Pick mason jars that have a two-piece closure. (The closure should consist of a reusable band and lid.) The lid should be discarded after every use because it can't reseal a jar effectively. If the food doesn't seal right, it may become home to dangerous bacteria. Since mason jars are glass, you should make sure to always inspect them before use. Any slight crack can let in harmful bacteria or break and contaminate the food with glass. Neither is going to be fun to digest. Most canners will suggest using Ball or Kerr brands as they are sturdy and tend to last the longest.

Lastly, you'll be needing a jar lifter. You may feel like this is unnecessary but trust me, after a couple of burns you'll learn your lesson. Jar lifters are just large tongs that can take the jars in and out of the canner. Remember, the water bath canner reaches temperatures of 212 °F. You do not want your hand anywhere near that even after it's cooled. Some other helpful, but not as mandatory, utensils you might need are a ladle and funnel. Ladles are great for spooning ingredients into the jars, while funnels help do the same thing and limit any spilling that might occur.

Choosing a Canning Recipe

This book contains 60 canning recipes for you to use. The easiest place to start is with a simple canned fruit recipe. There are a couple to choose from in Chapter 4's "Fruit" section. You don't have to start there, though. If you're a talented cook, you might be interested in checking out Chapter 3, where I've compiled several jelly, jam, marmalade, and chutney recipes. When it comes to water bath canning, these types of recipes are the most used. If you want to show off your work as a beginner, or even a canning veteran, this is definitely the way to go. Another easy way to leave an impression is by making a pie filling. The dessert is an American classic and with so many options it's a delicious start to your canning pantry.

Before you choose a recipe, you should know what you're looking for. A recipe may sound fun to make but are you actually going to eat it? If you plan on selling your canned goods, do you know what types are most popular on the market right now? Don't get excited and start canning everything you can. It's worse to can things and end up throwing them away than to just throw something away from the start. You waste time and energy by canning them first. (You get experience, too, but it's not really worth it if you can't enjoy your progress.) If you want to start with big loads, you can just make sure to use it all.

While I have spent a great deal of time finding these recipes, I'm not going to take it personally if you decide you want to try a recipe not found within this book. Finding and choosing your own recipes is an important part of your canning journey. Everyone has their own preferred diet and nutritional needs. Your recipes should reflect that. For example, many of the recipes in this book contain sugar because it's an important part of the water bath canning process. If you're more focused on a lower-calorie diet, you'll need to find recipes that use sugar alternatives. Canners with more experience usually end up substituting their own preferred ingredients into recipes to make it their own.

If you're going to find your own recipes, choose wisely. The internet is a limitless place to start but there are a lot of unreliable sources out there. It's up to you to find safe canning practices. Always double check that what is being canned can be safely processed in your water bath canner. The best way to do this is to research the USDA's canning guidelines. If a recipe is directly contradicting these guidelines then it's definitely not safe. You can always contact your local extension service to find safe recipes that match your chosen diet as well. It's also important to find recipes that work for the amount you want to make. Some processing times change depending on whether you have pints or quarts. You don't want to end up with an under or over-processed product.

Other Helpful Tips

Canning should be fun. If you're not having fun then you're probably not doing it correctly. The best way in my opinion to do this is to not can alone. A canning partner can help you find fun new recipes, challenge you to try something new, and just add a level of excitement you might not have alone. Canning can even be a friendly competition; see whose apple pie filling comes out better, learn from each other, and evolve faster in your canning journey. It can also just be a great bonding experience with siblings, a parent, a child, or a friend. Canning is a fulfilling experience and what could be better than sharing that achievement with a loved one.

Another tip is to only use the freshest of ingredients. Frozen food isn't going to result in high-quality canned goods. The flavor will certainly never match its fresh counterparts. Will it taste unbearably bad? No, but it's just a watered-down version now. If you are putting all of this work into learning, preparing, planning and creating, don't you want the best possible outcome? There isn't any need to preserve frozen fruit. The whole point of canning fruit is to keep it fresh so you can enjoy it in seasons it's not available. Frozen fruit can be found in the grocery aisle whenever. At that point, opening a jar of something that you can just go to the grocery and get loses its magic.

My favorite way to get fresh fruits is to go out and pick them myself. You can get perfectly healthy fruit at a farmer's market for a fair price and there's nothing wrong with that; I do this all the time. However, the experience of apple picking is unmatched. Maybe it's just the giddiness of the season, but the smell of fresh apples and the abundance of choices just makes my heart melt. There's also an unspoken beauty in picking blueberries from a wild bush. Orchard picking isn't something I get to do a lot of, but I certainly suggest trying it, just for the experience, at least once on your canning journey.

Another way to make sure you have fresh ingredients is to grow them yourself. Starting a garden for your canned goods is a whole other journey, one that is just as fulfilling and a little more aesthetic. Not everyone has the space or the time for a home garden and that's okay. There are plenty of other ways to get fresh produce. If you are lucky enough to have the space and time, start off small with some strawberries. Just grow a little batch and use them for canning. It's a great way to test the waters without diving in.

Key Chapter 1 Takeaways

- Water bath canning is a canning method for food with high acid.
- Low-acid food should only be preserved in a pressure canner.
- Make sure you have clean and working equipment before you start canning.
- Make sure your recipe is USDA approved and follows their health and safety protocols.
- For the best results when canning, use the freshest ingredients.

Chapter 2
How to Water Bath Can in 4 Easy Steps

"Every journey begins with a single step."

-Maya Angelou

Step 1: Preparation

The first thing you should always do before starting to can is clean. Clean absolutely everything from the jars to the canner itself. This may seem like overkill and it absolutely is. A good philosophy to have when it comes to canning is that it's better to be safe than sorry. If your utensils have been sitting in storage for half a year, it's likely to have accumulated some dust. You won't want to pour food into dusty jars. Not only could it be dangerous for bacterial reasons but it's not very appetizing either. When you are done washing all of your equipment make sure to thoroughly dry it off.

While a canner's worst fear is botulism, a canner's worst enemy is rust. Cleaning your equipment before use is a great time to check it over for any possible rust. Rust can ruin the integrity of the canner and cause holes where you don't want them. Canners are supposed to last decades if they are properly maintained. The last thing you'll want to do is have to replace your expensive equipment because it's faulty. This is why canners need to be stored in a similar location to the canned goods. The right conditions will keep it safe from any possible rust or even mold.

If the process time for your goods is less than 10 minutes you'll need to sterilize the jars. To do this, place the empty jars in the water bath canner right side up and fill the canner with water. This should come to about 1 inch above the jars. Boil the water for 10 minutes. (Add one minute every 1,000 feet above sea level where you are located.) When this is done, remove the jars from the canner using a jar lifter. Drain the hot water from the jars and dry them off before adding food. You can leave the water in the canner and use it to process the food.

If you don't need to sterilize the jars, you still need to make sure they are warm before the food goes in them. In this case you can fill the water bath canner ⅓ of the way. Place the jars upside down and let the steam keep them warm. (You can also just wash them in a dishwasher and keep them in there until you're ready to use them.) The lids and screw bands should also be warm. An easy way to do this is to put them in a warm bowl of water.

Step 2: Heating

After you have filled the jars and checked them for air bubble, it's time to put them in the canner. Using a jar lifter, slowly place the jars of food into the water bath canner. Evenly space them out on the rack so they aren't touching. The rack should assist with this. If you have a water bath canner, your rack should be able to rest on the sides of your canner. Once your rack is loaded, you can lower it down so the water is now covering the jar lids. Add water until there are 2 inches of water above the jars. It's important for the process that the water can freely move around the jars.

The time doesn't start until the canner is at a boil. When this starts to happen place the lid over the canner and have it come to a full rolling boil. It's best to measure the cooking time exactly so use an app on your phone or an actual kitchen timer. You'll definitely want an alarm if the process is going to take more than half an hour. If you choose to just pay attention to the clock you may accidentally over-process the food. The canner is going to reach temperatures of 212 °F, so make sure you don't accidentally burn yourself on the canister.

BOILING WATER BATH CANNING
Altitude Adjustment Chart

ALTITUDE	IF YOUR PROCESSING TIME IS LESS THAN 20 MINUTES	IF YOUR PROCESSING TIME IS MORE THAN 20 MINUTES
1,001 - 3,000 ft (305 - 914 m)	add 5 minutes to processing time	add 5 minutes to processing time
3,001 - 6,000 ft (915 - 1828 m)	add 10 minutes to processing time	add 5 minutes to processing time
6,001 ft and up (1829 m +)	add 15 minutes to processing time	add 10 minutes to processing time

Processing times can change depending on your altitude. Most recipes only provide the processing times for locations under 1,000 feet above sea level. If you live in high altitude places like Colorado, this could be a problem. The reason why altitude can affect processing times is because of the change in atmospheric pressure. By every 1,000 feet, the atmospheric pressure is reduced. This will make water boil at a lower temperature than 212 °F. Since water is boiling at a lower temperature, it's going to take longer to cook. It's important to research your altitude before you begin canning and change the processing times accordingly.

If you have a long processing time, it is vital for the canner to keep up the boiling. Every once in a while lift up the lid and look inside to make sure the canner is doing its job. The pot is supposed to be full of boiling water though, so be very careful. If you've noticed that the water is no longer at a full rolling boil, add some more boiling water to the canner to help it maintain its process. Be careful when adding in the boiling water, as you don't want to spill any and end up with any serious burns.

Step 3: Cooling

Once your timer goes off you can turn the heat off. The water bath canner will still be hot so be careful as you lift up the rack. Always wear protective gear around a heated water bath canner. You don't need goggles or anything dramatic like that, but oven mitts are a must have. Make sure not to shake the jars too much when you are lifting up the rack. The sealing process is still relatively fragile at this stage and you could mess it up. Before you take the jars out, give them a minute or two to cool down.

Grab your trusty jar lifters and slowly take the jars out one by one. The jars are still going to be very hot so make sure to put them on a wooden board or thick towel. You don't want to end up with any scorch marks on your counter. The jars should be in an upright position, as putting them in any other position will mess with the sealing process. There also needs to be a couple of inches between the jars so that air can freely circulate around them. Make sure they aren't located in a spot with a draft; cold air could break the hot glass of the jars and ruin all of your hard work.

In the next couple of minutes the jars will start to cool. As they do this the sealing process begins. You'll most likely hear a pop. This comes from the seal of the inner lid being pulled down and resulting in a satisfying "ping" sound. Make sure not to touch the jars during this cooling process. The worst thing you can do at this point is to press down on the lid. It will mess up the seal and make all of your hard work for nothing. The jars should be left alone for about 24 hours.

After the 24 hours of waiting comes the moment of truth. Press down on the lid to see if the sealing process was a success. If you find that the lid is sucked down and does not pop back up when you press down, congratulations—you did it! If it does pop up, it's not that big of a deal. The seal may not have worked but the food is still good. Just put it in the refrigerator and eat it in the next few days. You could also try to re-process it, but that might result in an overcooked taste and texture.

Step 4: Storing

Before you start canning you should already know where you are going to put your canned goods. Canned food needs a cool and dry environment to stay preserved. This can be a cellar or a temperature-controlled garage. It can also be a regular pantry; just make sure there is no direct sunlight. Another huge issue is using a location with any sort of humidity. If you're storing your canned goods in a cellar, there can't be any hot pipes around. This can result in steam that will pop the sealed lid straight off. Your location should also have enough room for your cans to stay organized. If you make more cans than your space allows, you could end up having to store them in a place that isn't ideal, and lose produce.

Once you have a location, it's time to store your first batch. Make sure to take off the screw band. This won't affect the actual seal and the lid will stay put. The problem with keeping the screw band on is that it could rust over and ruin your jar. It can also make it impossible to open the container safely. If you're having trouble removing a screw band, it's not the end of the world. Just keep it on and check on it every once in a while to make sure no rust is forming. If you try to force it, it can ruin the seal.

After removing the screw bands you're not yet done. The jars need to be labeled. I suggest adding the date that they were canned, the type of food in them, and any ingredients that went into them. The ingredient list might only seem necessary if you're planning on selling the goods, but it can come in handy even if you're not; when you're trying out different recipes, you want to know which ingredients worked best for you. When you are putting on the date, the year is just as important. You don't want to accidentally eat something that's seven years old. It won't kill you but it probably won't taste good.

The USDA recommends eating your canned goods within a year. After this point, the food quality will go down. You'll end up missing out on the nutritional value along with the taste. (However, in the case of an apocalypse, you may be happy you saved strawberries from 30 years ago.) So ultimately the decision whether to throw the food away after it has peaked is up to you. When you're done with a jar, make sure to discard the lid, wash the jar, and store it somewhere safe for the next harvest season.

Key Chapter 2 Takeaways

- Always wash all equipment between uses.
- Always use a jar lifter to prevent injury when removing and placing jars.
- The water in a boiling water bath canner should rise 2 inches above the jars.
- After canning, let the jars sit for 24 hours; messing with the lids before this time can result in an unsealed jar.
- Store jars in a cool and dry location for best results.

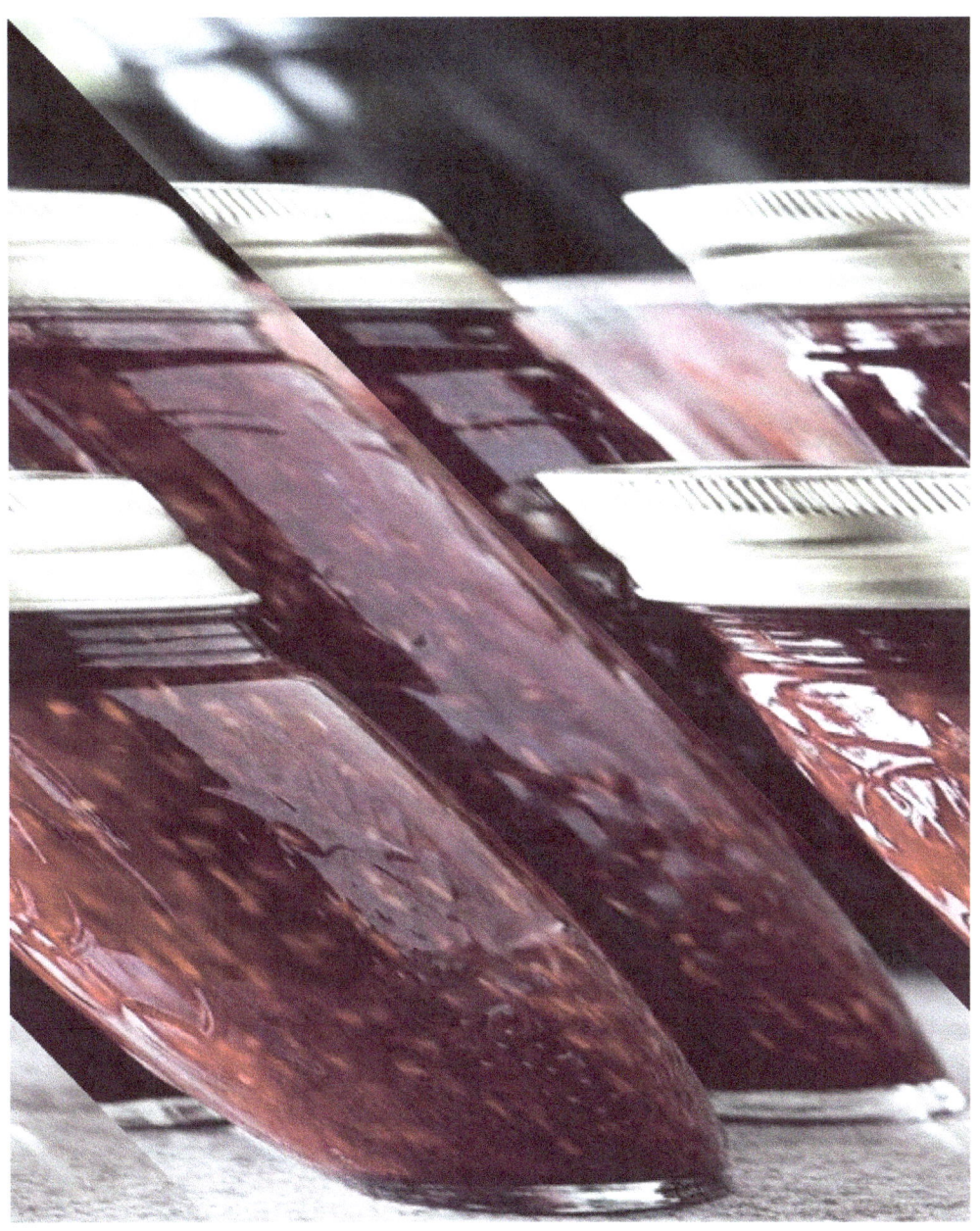

Chapter 3
Jams, Marmalades, Chutneys, and Jellies

"If life gives you the wobbles, make jelly."

- Magdalena VandenBerg

Jam Recipes

Straw-Berry Good Jam

Straw-Berry Good jam is a healthier alternative to sugar-packed store options. This jam uses honey instead of granulated sugar to sweeten, which infuses it with the honey's antioxidants and anti-inflammatory properties. Honey is also less processed than granulated sugar. The best time to prepare Straw-berry Good Jam is in June, when the berries are in peak season, depending on where you live: for example, strawberry season starts earlier in southern states.

Amount: Two 8 oz jars.

Ingredients: *(See page 172 for Measurement Conversion)*

- 1 ⅓ cups crushed strawberries
- ⅓ cup unsweetened fruit juice
- 1 ½ tablespoons No-Sugar Needed Pectin
- ⅓ cup honey

Directions:

1. Prepare all of the equipment. Wash the jars and sterilize them if necessary. Add water to the canner but wait to boil.
2. In a large saucepan, mix the strawberries and fruit juice at a low setting.
3. Then gradually add and stir in the Pectin to the mix.
4. After this, add the honey and raise the heat to high. Once it reaches a boil, maintain stirring for one minute before removing the pan from the heat source.
5. Funnel the hot jam into a heated jar leaving a ¼ inch of space before wiping the jar's rim and putting on the lid.
6. Using a jar lifter, gently place the jars in the canner, making sure there are 1-2 inches of water above them.
7. Bring the canner to a boil and let it process for 10 minutes. (Adjust time for altitude differences.)
8. After the time is up, turn off the heat and remove the canner's lid. Let it stand for five minutes before removal.
9. To remove the jars, use your jar lifter and let them cool for 24 hours before checking the seal.
10. Enjoy your Straw-Berry Good jam!

Apple-Solutely Delicious Jam

In regards to what type of apples to use for this jam, remember that jams are a lot like pies. You'll want an apple that won't crumble but will still have its sweet flavor. I recommend Granny Smith, Pink Ladies, or Honeycrisp apples. No matter what apple or combination of apples you use, you'll want the freshest ingredients. Apple-picking season is typically from August to October. Trust me, there is no better way to spend a beautiful fall day than in an apple orchard. While Apple-Solutely Delicious Jam isn't sugar-free, it is still a great addition to your breakfast toast.

Amount: Two half-pint jars.

Ingredients: *(See page 172 for Measurement Conversion)*

- 8 cups of diced apples
- 2 cups of sugar
- ¼ cup of lemon juice

Directions:

- Before your jam can be prepared, all of the ingredients must be mixed together in a covered container and be left in the refrigerator for 12 hours to marinate. This will help the jam keep its texture.
- After this waiting period, prepare all of the equipment. Wash the jars and sterilize them if necessary. Add water to the canner but wait to boil.
- In a large saucepan, heat the mixture to a boil on high.

- Stir for 20-30 minutes until the mixture has gelled. At sea level, the mixture will gel at 220 °F. Every 500 feet above sea level the temperature will be 1 degree lower than this. (For instance, at 1,000 feet, the jam will gel at 218 °F.)

- When the mixture has gelled, remove the saucepan from the heat source.

- Funnel the hot jam into a heated jar leaving a ¼ inch of space before wiping the jar's rim and putting on the lid.

- Using a jar lifter, gently place the jars in the canner, making sure there are 1-2 inches of water above them.
  Bring the canner to a boil and let it process for 10 minutes. Adjust time for altitude differences. After the time is up, turn off the heat and remove the canner's lid. Let it stand for five minutes before removal.

- To remove the jars, use your jar lifter and let them cool for 24 hours before checking the seal.

Enjoy your Apple-Solutely Delicious jam!

If You Like Piña Coladas Jam

This is a grown-up alternative to the previous jam recipes. With the special ingredient of rum, it will make a nice addition to brunch with your friends. While you can still find whole pineapples available at your local grocery store throughout the year, the fruit is more often imported to the U.S. than grown here. Even the United States' largest distributor, Hawaii, isn't on the mainland. Since the majority of the pineapples sold in the U.S. are from the West Indies or the Bahamas, finding the freshest ingredients just isn't possible. This jam is more of a fun treat than a dietary staple.

Amount: Five half pint jars

Ingredients: *(See page 172 for Measurement Conversion)*

- 2 cups fresh pureed pineapple
- ⅝ cup cream of coconut
- ¼ cup white rum
- ¼ cup lemon juice
- 3 cups sugar
- 1 ⅔ ounces of liquid pectin

Directions:

- Prepare all of the equipment. Wash the jars and sterilize them if necessary. Add water to the canner but wait to boil.
- In a large saucepan, mix the pineapple, cream of coconut, rum, and lemon juice together. Stir in the sugar.
- Bring the mixture to a boil on high heat and stir it for three minutes.
- Remove the saucepan from the heat source and add in the pectin. Make sure to skim off any foam that may form.

- Funnel the hot jam into a heated jar leaving a ¼ inch of space before wiping the jar's rim and putting on the lid.

- Using a jar lifter, gently place the jars in the canner, making sure there are 1-2 inches of water above them.

- Bring the canner to a boil and let it process for five minutes. Adjust time for altitude differences.

- After the time is up, turn off the heat and remove the canner's lid. Let it stand for five minutes before removal.

- To remove the jars, use your jar lifter and let them cool for 24 hours before checking the seal.

- Enjoy your If You Like Piña Coladas jam!

Marmalade Recipes

Orange You Glad Marmalade

With any orange-based recipe, we must ask ourselves the inevitable question: Florida or California. It all depends on what you are looking for. Florida oranges may have the sweeter taste, but California has a thicker peel. Interestingly, the oranges that are typically used in marmalade, Seville oranges, are not even mass produced in the United States. The most popular oranges are Navel and Valencia. It all comes down to preference, and most kinds of oranges will hold up. The best time to make this marmalade is from November to May, during peak harvest season.

Amount: Six half pint jars

Ingredients: *(See page 172 for Measurement Conversion)*

- 3 oranges
- 3 cups water
- ¼ cup of lemon juice
- 4 ¾ cups of granulated sugar
- 2 tablespoons of pectin

Directions:

1. Thinly slice the oranges with the skin on, cutting off the bottom and top stems. Cut the slices again into four pieces.
2. In a large stockpot, mix the lemon juice, oranges, and water, and bring to a boil before letting it simmer for one hour. Stir when needed.

3. Prepare all of the equipment. Wash the jars and sterilize them if necessary. Add water to the canner but wait to boil.
4. Once the peel is tender, mix in the pectin and bring the pot to a rolling boil again. Then stir in all of the sugar at once and return to a boil, this time for four minutes, before removing the pot from the heat source and skimming off any excess foam.
5. Funnel the marmalade into a heated jar leaving ⅛ inch of space before wiping the jar's rim and putting on the lid.
6. Using a jar lifter, gently place the jars in the canner, making sure there are 1-2 inches of water above them.
7. Bring the canner to a boil and let it process for 10 minutes. Adjust time for altitude differences.
8. After the time is up, turn off the heat and remove the canner's lid. Let it stand for five minutes before removal.
9. To remove the jars, use your jar lifter and let them cool for 24 hours before checking the seal.
10. Enjoy your Orange You Glad marmalade!

Simply the Zest Lemon Marmalade

Simply the Zest marmalade is an easy two-ingredient recipe perfect for marmalade on a budget. While most recipes won't actually call for a specific lemon, Bearss lemons are the most common to find in the U.S., growing in places like California and Arizona. The best thing about Simply the Zest lemon marmalade is that you don't have to wait to make it. Lemons are unique in the fact that the trees can bloom all year round. The only lemon with a peak season is the Meyer lemon that is harvested from November to April.

Amount: Five half pint jars

Ingredients: *(See page 172 for Measurement Conversion)*

- 3 lbs of fresh lemons
- 2 cups of sugar

Directions:

1. Cut the lemon in half and juice the halves. Save the juice for later use. Next, thinly slice the lemon halves.
2. Prepare all of the equipment. Wash the jars and sterilize them if necessary. Add water to the canner but wait to boil.
3. In a large stockpot, boil the lemon slices for 10-15 minutes. Once the peels are tender, drain and rinse the lemons.
4. In a clean pot, add water to the lemons and bring to a boil. Stir in the sugar and let simmer for an hour.
5. Add ½ cup of lemon juice from the squeezed lemons before removing the mixture from the heat source.
6. Remove the lemon pits before funneling the marmalade into a heated jar, leaving ¼ inch of space. Wipe the jar's rim and put on the lid.
7. Using a jar lifter, gently place the jars in the canner, making sure there are 1-2 inches of water above them.

8. Bring the canner to a boil and let it process for 15 minutes. Adjust time for altitude differences.
9. After the time is up, turn off the heat and remove the canner's lid. Let it stand for five minutes before removal. To remove the jars, use your jar lifter and let them cool for 24 hours before checking the seal.
10. Enjoy your Simply the Zest lemon marmalade!

Sub-Lime Marmalade

While Sub-Lime marmalade is another easy-to-make recipe, garden-fresh ingredients might not be on the table. The United States' climate is not suitable for lime production, so the majority of our commercially sold limes are imported from Mexico. However, you can grow your own in an indoor container. Peak season for limes is usually from May to October, but homegrown limes aren't affected by the climate and can be harvested anytime. Sub-Lime marmalade is certainly worth the investment.

Amount: Five half pint jars

Ingredients: *(See page 172 for Measurement Conversion)*

- 5 peeled Persian limes, zest should be cut into 2 inch strips
- 3 ½ cups of sugar
- 2 ¼ cups of water

Directions:

1. To start, cut the lime in half and juice the halves. Save the juice to use later. Next, scrape out the pulp and seeds from the lime halves and place them in a cheese bag.
2. In a large saucepan, cover and soak the cheese bag, zest, and juice for eight hours.
3. Prepare all of the equipment. Wash the jars and sterilize them if necessary. Add water to the canner but wait to boil.
4. Cook the mixture for 30 minutes or until the peels have softened.
5. Remove the cheese bag and add the sugar. Once the sugar has dissolved, boil the mixture until 220 °F.
6. Funnel the marmalade into a heated jar, leaving ¼ inch of space. Wipe the jar's rim and put on the lid. Using a jar lifter, gently place the jars in the canner, making sure there are 1-2 inches of water above them.
7. Bring the canner to a boil and let it process for 10 minutes. Adjust time for altitude differences.
8. After the time is up, turn off the heat and remove the canner's lid. Let it stand for five minutes before removal.
9. To remove the jars, use your jar lifter and let them cool for 24 hours before checking the seal.
10. Enjoy your Sub-Lime marmalade!

Chutney Recipes

It Takes Two to Mango Chutney

Mango chutney is a traditional Indian dish. Once again I'm substituting honey for sugar here, but if you want a more customary result, you can always use 2 cups of sugar instead. While the mango, similar to the recipe, may have originated from India, mangoes are grown in the United States in the warm climate of Florida. Peak harvest season is from May through September. Imported mangoes from Asia are available all year round.

Amount: Six half pint jars

Ingredients: *(See page 172 for Measurement Conversion)*

- 1 ½ cups of honey
- 1 cup of distilled white vinegar
- 6 cups of mangoes, peeled and cut in ¾ -inch pieces
- 1 cup of chopped onion
- ½ cup of golden raisins
- ¼ cup of crystallized ginger, finely chopped
- 1 garlic clove, minced
- 1 teaspoon mustard seeds, whole
- ¼ teaspoon red chili pepper flakes

Directions:

1. Prepare all of the equipment and ingredients. Wash the jars and sterilize them if necessary. Add water to the canner but wait to boil.
2. In a large pot, mix the honey and vinegar together and set to boil.
3. Add all of the remaining ingredients into the mixture and set to simmer for 45 minutes to an hour. Stir when needed.
4. Once the chutney has slightly thickened and reached its syrupy texture, remove the mixture from the heat source.
5. Funnel the chutney into a heated jar, leaving ½ inch of space. Wipe the jar's rim and put on the lid.
6. Using a jar lifter, gently place the jars in the canner, making sure there are 1-2 inches of water above them.
7. Bring the canner to a boil and let it process for 15 minutes. Adjust time for altitude differences.
8. After the time is up, turn off the heat and remove the canner's lid. Let it stand for five minutes before removal.
9. To remove the jars, use your jar lifter and let them cool for 24 hours before checking the seal.
10. Enjoy your chutney!

Peachy Keen Chutney

Peach chutneys are generally a more Western-style version of a traditional Indian dish. Despite the fact that the state of Georgia is nicknamed the "Peach State," California is the largest contributor of the fruit in the United States. Attaining fresh and local peaches for your chutney will be easy since more than 20 states commercially produce them. The peak harvest season for peaches is usually from May to September, but since the fruit is so widely grown in the U.S. it's available multiple times throughout the year.

Amount: Five half pint jars

Ingredients: *(See page 172 for Measurement Conversion)*

- 3 pounds of peaches
- 1 ¼ cups of light brown sugar
- 1 ½ cups of apple cider vinegar
- 1 cup of golden raisins
- 1 small lemon, seeded and finely chopped, including peel
- ¼ cup fresh ginger, finely chopped
- 1 medium onion, peeled and finely chopped
- 1 small hot chili pepper, finely chopped
- ½ teaspoon salt
- ¼ teaspoon ground allspice
- ¼ teaspoon freshly ground black pepper
- ¼ teaspoon ground coriander

Directions:

1. Blanch the peaches for easy skin removal and then chop them up into ½ inch chunks.
2. Prepare all of the equipment. Wash the jars and sterilize them if necessary. Add water to the canner but wait to boil.
3. In a large pot, combine all of the ingredients and cook over high heat until the peaches are soft.

4. If the chutney seems too liquidy, raise the heat to thicken it. Once you've reached an ideal texture remove the mixture from the heat source.
5. Funnel the chutney into a heated jar, leaving ½ inch of space. Wipe the jar's rim and put on the lid.
6. Using a jar lifter, gently place the jars in the canner, making sure there are 1-2 inches of water above them.
7. Bring the canner to a boil and let it process for 10 minutes. Adjust time for altitude differences.
8. After the time is up, turn off the heat and remove the canner's lid. Let it stand for five minutes before removal.
9. To remove the jars, use your jar lifter and let them cool for 24 hours before checking the seal.
10. Enjoy your Peachy Keen chutney!

Pear-Fect Chutney

Pear chutney is another traditional Indian dish. The majority of commercially sold pears are grown on the west coast in states such as California, Oregon, or Washington. Similarly to apples, pears can be harvested in orchards from August to October, and make great plans for a lovely fall day. While planting your own pear tree won't take a lot of maintenance, the crop can take years to yield any results.

Amount: Five half pint jars

Ingredients: *(See page 172 for Measurement Conversion)*

- 3 pounds pears, peeled, cored, and chopped
- 1 ¼ cups of light brown sugar
- 1 ½ cups of apple cider vinegar
- 1 1/2 cups of raisins
- 1 lemon, seeded and finely chopped
- 1/4 cup fresh ginger, peeled and finely chopped
- 1 clove garlic, peeled and finely chopped
- 1 small hot chile pepper, finely chopped
- 1/2 teaspoon kosher salt
- 1/4 teaspoon allspice
- 1/4 teaspoon ground black pepper
- 1/4 teaspoon ground coriander
- Pinch ground cloves

Directions:

1. Prepare the pears by washing them before they are cored, peeled, and chopped.
2. Prepare all the equipment. Wash the jars and sterilize them if necessary. Add water to the canner but wait to boil.
3. In a large pot, combine all of the ingredients and cook over high heat until the pears are soft. Stir regularly.
4. If the chutney seems too liquidy, raise the heat to thicken it. Once you've reached an ideal texture remove the mixture from the heat source.
5. Funnel the chutney into a heated jar, leaving ½ inch of space. Wipe the jar's rim and put on the lid.

6. Using a jar lifter, gently place the jars in the canner, making sure there are 1-2 inches of water above them.
7. Bring the canner to a boil and let it process for 10 minutes. Adjust time for altitude differences.
8. After the time is up, turn off the heat and remove the canner's lid. Let it stand for five minutes before removal.
9. To remove the jars, use your jar lifter and let them cool for 24 hours before checking the seal.
10. Enjoy your Pear-Fect chutney!

Jelly Recipes

Be Grape-Ful Jelly

Grapes are popularly grown throughout the United States, but once again California takes the cake for the biggest commercial producer of this fruit. When it comes to choosing what grape to use in your jelly, I would suggest Concord for their sweet taste and aroma. If you grow your own grapes, make sure not to use wine grapes as they have a rather bitter flavor that doesn't really work for jelly. Grape harvest season peaks from August to October.

Amount: Eight pint jars

Ingredients: *(See page 172 for Measurement Conversion)*

- 3 ½ of pounds Concord grapes
- ½ cup of water
- 7 cups of white sugar

- 6 ounces of liquid pectin

Directions:

1. Wash and remove stems from the grapes before crushing them. In a large pot, bring the grapes to a boil. Let the mixture simmer for 10 minutes before removing the heat source and straining the juice. Refrigerate the juice for 12 hours.

2. Prepare all of the canning equipment. Wash the jars and sterilize them if necessary. Add water to the canner but wait to boil.

3. After the juice has cooled, strain it again through a double-thickness damp cheesecloth. This should result in four cups of juice.

4. Mix juice and sugar in a large pot before bringing it to a rolling boil.

5. Stir in the pectin and boil it for one minute before removing the jelly from the heat source. Skim off foam.

6. Funnel the jelly into a heated jar, leaving ¼ inch of space. Wipe the jar's rim and put on the lid. Using a jar lifter, gently place the jars in the canner, making sure there are 1-2 inches of water above them.

7. Bring the canner to a boil and let it process for five minutes. Adjust time for altitude differences.

8. After the time is up, turn off the heat and remove the canner's lid. Let it stand for five minutes before removal.

9. To remove the jars, use your jar lifter and let them cool for 24 hours before checking the seal.

Dandy Dandelion Jelly

Whether or not you consider dandelions a weed or a flower, they sure do make good jelly. One of my favorite things about dandelions is that they grow just about anywhere there is grass. They are also cost-effective since they are so abundant. The best time to find dandelions is in the spring, but they do bloom in the fall as well. Dandelion picking can be a fun activity for the family. Just remember you only need the flowers, not the stems.

Amount: Five half pint jars

Ingredients: *(See page 172 for Measurement Conversion)*

- 2 cups of dandelion petals, lightly packed
- 4 cups of water
- 4 cups of sugar

- 2 tablespoons of lemon juice
- 1 box powdered pectin

Directions:

1. Remove all of the green parts from the dandelions and put the petals in a quart jar.
2. Pour 4 cups of boiling water over the flowers. Once the jar has cooled down, refrigerate for 24 hours.
3. Prepare all the equipment. Wash the jars and sterilize them if necessary. Add water to the canner but wait to boil.
4. Strain dandelions and squeeze out any remaining tea before discarding them. This should result in a little less than 4 cups of dandelion tea.
5. Boil the tea with lemon juice and pectin in a large pot.
6. Add sugar and bring the mixture back to a boil for two minutes before removing the jelly from its heat source.
7. Funnel the jelly into a heated jar, leaving ¼ inch of space. Wipe the jar's rim and put on the lid. Using a jar lifter, gently place the jars in the canner, making sure there are 1-2 inches of water above them.
8. Bring the canner to a boil and let it process for 10 minutes. Adjust time for altitude differences.
9. After the time is up, turn off the heat and remove the canner's lid. Let it stand for five minutes before removal. To remove the jars, use your jar lifter and let them cool for 24 hours before checking the seal.

Plum Out of Puns Jelly

I promise this is the last fruit-related pun. Wild plum trees are highly adaptable, and that is why they can grow all across the United States. From Massachusetts to New Mexico, this plant is best used for jelly or other byproducts since it's flavor isn't always consistent. Growing your own plum tree won't be hard to maintain as long as it has enough sunlight. Late May to August is peak harvest for these versatile fruits.

Amount: Four pint jars

Ingredients: *(See page 172 for Measurement Conversion)*

- 5 pounds of ripe plums
- 1 ½ cups of water
- 1.75 ounces of pectin
- 1 Tablespoons of unsalted butter
- 6 ½ cups of sugar

Directions:

1. Plums should be pitted and cut in half. Peeling is unnecessary.
2. Prepare all the canning equipment. Wash the jars and sterilize them if necessary. Add water to the canner but wait to boil.
3. In a large pot, add the water to the plums and bring it to a boil. Cover the pot and let it simmer for 10 minutes.
4. Use a fine mesh strainer to strain the juice. Let this drain for 30 minutes before discarding the fruit. This should result in 5 ½ cups of fruit juice.

5. Pour the juice back into the pot and add the butter and pectin. Bring this mixture to a rolling boil.
6. Add the sugar and boil for one minute before removing the jelly from the heat source. Skim off any foam.
7. Funnel the jelly into a heated jar, leaving ¼ inch of space. Wipe the jar's rim and put on the lid. Using a jar lifter, gently place the jars in the canner, making sure there are 1-2 inches of water above them.
8. Bring the canner to a boil and let it process for 10 minutes. Adjust time for altitude differences. After the time is up, turn off the heat and remove the canner's lid. Let it stand for five minutes before removal.
9. To remove the jars, use your jar lifter and let them cool for 24 hours before checking the seal.

Key Chapter 3 Takeaways

- Jam, marmalade, chutney, and jelly are all different ways to prepare and preserve fruit.
- Different harvest seasons affect when to get the freshest fruit.
- Fruit grows all across the United States but most can be found in California due to the warm climate.
- The best ingredient in any jam, marmalade, chutney, or jelly is fresh fruit gardened at home or grown locally.
- Though many fruits can be grown locally, the United States doesn't have the climate for limes.

Chapter 4
Desserts

"Life is short and unpredictable. Eat the dessert first."

- Jacques Torres

Canning Desserts 101

Many of the main ingredients in common desserts are not eligible to be canned in any capacity whether it is a water bath canner or a pressure canner. Water bath canning is mostly just suitable for fruit-related desserts. This doesn't mean pies in their whole capacities though. Not only would it completely lose its shape in the jar, but grains can't be safely processed. The temperature in a water bath canner can't cook raw dough. Also, grains don't hold heat well enough to kill off bacteria, and canning them could result in botulism. This means any dessert that contains bread, rice, pie dough, biscuits, or crackers should not be canned. Pie filling is regularly canned, though, because it does not have any ingredients that aren't safe.

Any desserts that contain dairy products can not be canned at all either. Milk is so low in acid that even a pressure canner can't get rid of any possible botulism spores. Butter, cheese, and cream all have the same consequences as well. That means chocolate, whipped cream, yogurt parfaits, pudding, and cheesecake filling can't be preserved. This rule doesn't just apply to cow's milk either—no milk of any kind will work, including goat's milk. Soy and tofu have the same problem, and can't be used as alternatives. Dairy is healthier and better tasting if it is served fresh.

Other desserts that won't work are sweets such as caramel and marshmallow. The largest problem with these are the amount of fats they contain. Oftentimes, the fat will impede the sealing process, and the jar will be exposed to airborne bacteria. Even if the jar does seal, the fat will most likely spoil and will ruin the food since it won't properly cook. Any dessert ingredients with nuts, such as Nutella or peanut butter, have too much oil. The oil found in nuts protects botulism spores from the heating process.

When it comes to canning desserts there are a couple of ways you can substitute healthier options for sugar. You can use water instead of sugar and the process will still work; however, the fruit's shape won't hold as well. Honey has numerous health benefits, but it does have more calories. It's also sweeter, so you don't have to use as much. Calorie-wise, this kind of evens out, but unsweetened juice is a good lower-calorie option as well. If you are working with peaches, pears, apricots, plums, and red or white sweet cherries, then a diluted frozen apple juice concentrate will do the job. The artificial sweetener Splenda doesn't have preserving-properties like sugar does, and can't be used to pickle, but it won't affect jam or jelly.

Fruit Recipes

Blasting Blueberries

This recipe is a great place to start for beginner canners. You don't need many ingredients, just blueberries and water. Blueberries are often considered a superfood due to their numerous health benefits. This fruit is full of antioxidant compounds such as anthocyanin, which can help with heart disease. Once frozen, blueberries can lose these properties, so canning is the better option when it comes to preservation. Blueberries grow all over the United States and are easy to produce in home gardens. Peak harvest for this fruit is between June and August.

Amount: Two quarts

Ingredients: *(See page 172 for Measurement Conversion)*

- 2 quarts of fresh blueberries
- 6 cups of water

Directions:

1. Prepare all the canning equipment and wash and remove stems from fruit. Wash the jars and sterilize them if necessary. Add water to the canner but wait to boil.
2. Blanch the blueberries in small portions at 30 second intervals at a time.

3. Remove the blueberries from the pan using a sieve.
4. Once you are finished blanching, fill the quart jars with the blueberries, leaving room for blanching juice and ¼ inch of space at the top.
5. If you run out blanching liquid, boil water to fill the rest of the space.
6. Wipe the jar's rim and put on the lid. Using a jar lifter, gently place the jars in the canner, making sure there are 1-2 inches of water above them.
7. Bring the canner to a boil and let it process for 15 minutes. Adjust time for altitude differences.
8. After the time is up, turn off the heat and remove the canner's lid. Let it stand for five minutes before removal.
9. To remove the jars, use your jar lifter and let them cool for 24 hours before checking the seal.
10. Enjoy your Blasting Blueberries!

Rockin Raspberries

While this recipe isn't as healthy as the previous one, it's still an easy place to start on your canning journey. For your first recipe, you'll want to start with a short ingredients list that is easy to find, like raspberries and sugar. The small fruit require little to no preparation before they are placed in the jars. Raspberries, like most fruit in the U.S., are commercially grown on the west coast but they can make a great addition to any home garden. The best time to pick them is from July to early fall.

Amount: Six pint jars

Ingredients: *(See page 172 for Measurement Conversion)*

- 8 pints of fresh raspberries
- 2 ½ cups of sugar
- 6 cups of water

Directions:

1. Raspberries are small enough that they don't need to be chopped, but always wash the fruit before you begin.
2. Prepare all the canning equipment. Wash the jars and sterilize them if necessary. Add water to the canner but wait to boil.
3. Prepare syrup by bringing a mixture of sugar and water to a boil and then letting it simmer.
4. Pour syrup into hot jars and then add the raspberries. Gently shake the jars to make more room and a tighter pack.
5. Add more syrup if necessary and leave ¼ inch of space at the top of the jar. Make sure to get rid of any air bubbles.
6. Wipe the jar's rim and put on the lid. Using a jar lifter, gently place the jars in the canner, making sure there are 1-2 inches of water above them.
7. Bring the canner to a boil and let it process for 15 minutes. Adjust time for altitude differences.
8. After the time is up, turn off the heat and remove the canner's lid. Let it stand for five minutes before removal.

9. To remove the jars, use your jar lifter and let them cool for 24 hours before checking the seal.
10. Enjoy your Rockin Raspberries!

Krazy Kiwi

Despite their prickly texture, kiwis have a sweet taste. They will have a milder flavor after canning, though, and the color may fade as well. The Golden State, California, is the leading producer of this hairy fruit. Kiwis aren't the obvious choice for a home garden, but with a little care they can yield wonderful results. The U.S. kiwi season is from October through May.

Amount: Varies

Ingredients: *(See page 172 for Measurement Conversion)*

- Fresh kiwi
- 2 cups of sugar
- 4 cups of water

Directions:

1. Slice the kiwi in half and scoop out the inside. Cut the chunks any way you desire. I like to thinly slice them and turn the slices into fun shapes for a more aesthetic look.
2. Prepare all the canning equipment. Wash the jars and sterilize them if necessary. Add water to the canner but wait to boil.

3. In a pan, simmer the water and slowly add the sugar until it dissolves.
4. Gently boil the syrup for three minutes and make sure to keep the mixture warm before it goes into the jars.
5. Fill the jars with kiwi and then add the syrup, leaving ¼ inch of space.
6. Wipe the jar's rim and put on the lid. Using a jar lifter, gently place the jars in the canner, making sure there are 1-2 inches of water above them.
7. Bring the canner to a boil and let it process for 20 minutes. Adjust time for altitude differences.
8. After the time is up, turn off the heat and remove the canner's lid. Let it stand for five minutes before removal.
9. To remove the jars, use your jar lifter and let them cool for 24 hours before checking the seal.
10. Enjoy your Krazy Kiwi!

Pie Filling Recipes

Granny's Apple Pie Filling

This apple pie filling isn't actually my grandmother's recipe. The "granny" in the title refers to the Granny Smith apples I use to give the pie filling its sweet taste. Any pie apple will do in this recipe, but these apples are my personal recommendation. Granny Smiths are easy to obtain all year round, and work well when they are mixed with other pie apples, such as Honey Crisps or Pink Ladies. The filling is good to eat straight out of the jar into a precooked crust. (*Note: Some of these recipes use Clear Jel. Clear Jel is a chemically modified corn starch. It produces superb consistency even after your filling is baked or canned. It helps prevent your sauce becoming runny. It is popular in the USA but difficult to come by in other countries. Please research some suitable alternatives in your area. Substitutes that I have come across include Tapioca Starch and Gum Arabic Powder.*)

Amount: Seven pint jars

Ingredients: *(See page 172 for Measurement Conversion)*

- 12 cups of apple slices, peeled, cored, and splashed with lemon juice to prevent browning
- 2 ¾ cups of sugar
- ¾ cup of Clear Jel
- 1 teaspoon of ground cinnamon
- ½ teaspoon of ground nutmeg
- 1 ¼ cups of water
- 2 ½ cups of apple juice
- ½ cups lemon juice

Directions:

1. Prepare all the canning equipment. Wash the jars and sterilize them if necessary. Add water to the canner but wait to boil.

2. Blanch the apples in boiling water for one minute. Strain the apples and cover them to keep them warm.
3. Mix the water, sugar, Clear Jel, ground cinnamon, ground nutmeg, and apple juice in a large saucepan. Bring the mixture to a boil before adding the lemon juice. Return to a boil for one minute
4. Stir in the apples.
5. Funnel the filling into a heated jar, leaving 1 inch of space. Remove any air bubbles. Wipe the jar's rim and put on the lid.
6. Using a jar lifter, gently place the jars in the canner, making sure there are 1-2 inches of water above them.
7. Bring the canner to a boil and let it process for 25 minutes. Adjust time for altitude differences.
8. After the time is up, turn off the heat and remove the canner's lid. Let it stand for five minutes before removal.
9. To remove the jars, use your jar lifter and let them cool for 24 hours before checking the seal.
10. Enjoy your Granny's Apple Pie!

The Great Rhubarb Pie Filling

While this pie is great tasting, it is actually named after the empress of Russia, Catherine the Great. During her reign she banned the export of rhubarb seeds to give her country a monopoly over the root. Lucky for us, a Russian physician smuggled them into Europe, and now we have delicious rhubarb pie. Rhubarb grows anywhere in the U.S., but mostly comes from the northern west coast. The season for this vegetable starts in the spring and goes into early summer.

Amount: Two pint jars

Ingredients: *(See page 172 for Measurement Conversion)*

- 3½ cups of chopped rhubarb
- 1 cup of sugar
- ¼ cup of Clear Jel
- 4 tablespoons of lemon juice

Directions:

1. Prepare all the canning equipment. Wash the jars and sterilize them if necessary. Add water to the canner but wait to boil.
2. Mix the chopped rhubarb with sugar and let it sit for 15-30 minutes. Wait until juice appears.
3. Mix the Clear Jel and water before cooking it on medium. As soon as it thickens add the lemon juice and cook for one minute. Heat up the rhubarb separately.
4. Add the heated up rhubarb to the mixture and cook for three more minutes. Stir carefully as you go before finishing and removing it from the heat source.
5. Funnel the pie filling into a heated jar, leaving 1 inch of space. Wipe the jar's rim and put on the lid.

6. Using a jar lifter, gently place the jars in the canner, making sure there are 1-2 inches of water above them.
7. Bring the canner to a boil and let it process for 30 minutes. Adjust time for altitude differences.
8. After the time is up, turn off the heat and remove the canner's lid. Let it stand for five minutes before removal.
9. To remove the jars, use your jar lifter and let them cool for 24 hours before checking the seal.
10. Enjoy your Great Rhubarb Pie!

Cherry Bomb Pie Filling

This pie has an explosion of flavor. Get it? For the most part, sour cherries are more often used in pies than sweet ones. I prefer the juicier consistency, but if you want to use less sugar, you can always use sweet cherries to even out the taste. Cherries are grown throughout the U.S. and you could easily plant your own as long as you have sunlight and deep, well-drained soil. Depending on where in the States the cherries are coming from, the season differs. Peaks can be from anywhere between May and August.

(Note: This recipe use Clear Jel. Clear Jel is a chemically modified corn starch. It produces superb consistency even after your filling is baked or canned. It helps prevent your sauce becoming runny. It is popular in the USA but difficult to come by in other countries. Please research some suitable alternatives in your area. Substitutes that I have come across include Tapioca Starch and Gum Arabic Powder.)

Amount: Eight pint jars

Ingredients: *(See page 172 for Measurement Conversion)*

- 10 lbs of red cherries
- 3 ½ cups of sugar
- 1 cup of Clear Jel
- ½ teaspoon ground cinnamon
- ¼ cup of lemon juice

Directions:

1. Wash and strain the juice and remove any pits from the cherries. Keep at least 4 cups of juice for later.
2. Prepare all the canning equipment. Wash the jars and sterilize them if necessary. Add water to the canner but wait to boil.
3. In a large saucepan, mix cherry juice, sugar, Clear Jel, and cinnamon together and bring it to a boil.
4. Once thickened add lemon juice and return to boil.
5. Finally add the remaining cherries and return to boil again. Stir thoroughly.
6. Remove the sauce from the heat source and funnel the filling into a heated jar, leaving 1 inch of space. Wipe the jar's rim and put on the lid.
7. Using a jar lifter, gently place the jars in the canner, making sure there are 1-2 inches of water above them.

8. Bring the canner to a boil and let it process for 35 minutes. Adjust time for altitude differences. After the time is up, turn off the heat and remove the canner's lid. Let it stand for five minutes before removal.
9. To remove the jars, use your jar lifter and let them cool for 24 hours before checking the seal.
10. Enjoy your Cherry Bomb Pie Filling!

Fruit Sauce Recipes

Lemon Zest Blueberry Sauce

This sauce is one of my favorite additions to plain cheesecake, but if you're looking for a healthier way to use it, I also enjoy it with plain Greek yogurt. It's a great topping for breakfast foods such as waffles or pancakes, as well. For a quicker breakfast option, it pairs well with oatmeal. For a special treat, you can also use it as an ice cream topping. If you want more information on lemons or blueberries, you can find it in the Blasting Blueberries recipe from earlier in this chapter, or the Simply the Zest lemon marmalade recipe from Chapter 3.

Amount: Four pint jars

Ingredients: *(See page 172 for Measurement Conversion)*

- 8 cups of fresh blueberries

- 6 cups granulated sugar
- 2 teaspoon fresh lemon zest
- 2 tablespoon fresh lemon juice
- 6 ounces of pectin

Directions:

1. Prepare all the canning equipment. Wash the jars and sterilize them if necessary. Add water to the canner but wait to boil.
2. Slightly crush the blueberries without fully mashing them.
3. In a large pot, mix the berries, lemon juice, sugar, and lemon zest, and bring it to a rolling boil.
4. Add pectin then continue boiling for one minute. After you remove the sauce from the heat source, skim off any foam.
5. Funnel the sauce into a heated jar, leaving ¼ inch of space. Wipe the jar's rim and put on the lid.
6. Using a jar lifter, gently place the jars in the canner, making sure there are 1-2 inches of water above them.
7. Bring the canner to a boil and let it process for 10 minutes. Adjust time for altitude differences.
8. After the time is up, turn off the heat and remove the canner's lid. Let it stand for five minutes before removal.
9. To remove the jars, use your jar lifter and let them cool for 24 hours before checking the seal.
10. Enjoy your Lemon Zest Blueberry Sauce!

Awesomesauce Applesauce

This is a quick and easy applesauce recipe that I would consider to be a canning staple for any pantry. It saves a lot of time on cooking due to its versatility as a side. It goes with just about anything, but my recommendation is pork chops. It's also a blessing if you have young children or grandchildren. Even the most picky of eaters will enjoy this recipe. If you are curious about apple production in the U.S. more information is available in the Apple-Solutely Delicious Jam recipe in Chapter 3.

Amount: Six pints

Ingredients: *(See page 172 for Measurement Conversion)*

- 8 pounds tart cooking apples
- 2 cups of water
- 1 cup of sugar

Directions:

1. Prepare all the canning equipment. Wash the jars and sterilize them if necessary. Add water to the canner but wait to boil.
2. Prepare the apples by coring them and cutting them in quarters. Boil the apples in water and let simmer for 30 minutes or until tender.
3. Press the apples through a sieve or food mill.

4. Add the apple pulp back to the pot and stir in sugar. Add more water if necessary. Bring mixture to a boil.
5. Funnel the sauce into a heated jar, leaving ½ inch of space. Wipe the jar's rim and put on the lid.
6. Using a jar lifter, gently place the jars in the canner, making sure there are 1-2 inches of water above them.
7. Bring the canner to a boil and let it process for 15 minutes. Adjust time for altitude differences.
8. After the time is up, turn off the heat and remove the canner's lid. Let it stand for five minutes before removal.
9. To remove the jars, use your jar lifter and let them cool for 24 hours before checking the seal.
10. Enjoy your Awesomesauce Applesauce!

Cinnamon Pear Sauce

Pear sauce is great if you need an alternative to applesauce. Adding cinnamon to pear sauce gives the recipe just the slightest kick. The result is delicious. Cinnamon is one of my favorite ingredients to cook with due to its wonderful aroma, and this recipe is no different. If you want your home to smell like a cinnamon sugar dreamland, then I urge you to try it. Want to know more about pear production in the U.S.? Check out the Pear-Fect Chutney recipe in Chapter 3.

Amount: Three pints

Ingredients: *(See page 172 for Measurement Conversion)*

- 7 large pears, quartered and cored
- 1 juicy lemon, zested and juiced
- ¾ cup of water
- ¼ cup of white sugar
- ¼ teaspoon ground cinnamon

Directions:

1. Prepare all the canning equipment. Wash the jars and sterilize them if necessary. Add water to the canner but wait to boil.
2. In a large pan mix the lemon juice, zest and water. Slowly add in the pears as you cook. Simmer for 10 minutes or until the pears are tender.
3. Gently mash the pears and simmer for 10 more minutes.
4. Puree the mixture with either an immersion blender or a food mill.
5. Simmer puree and add sugar and cinnamon. Cook until desired consistency is attained.
6. Funnel the sauce into a heated jar, leaving ½ inch of space. Wipe the jar's rim and put on the lid.
7. Using a jar lifter, gently place the jars in the canner, making sure there are 1-2 inches of water above them.
8. Bring the canner to a boil and let it process for 10 minutes. Adjust time for altitude differences. After the time is up, turn off the heat and remove the canner's lid. Let it stand for five minutes before removal.

9. To remove the jars, use your jar lifter and let them cool for 24 hours before checking the seal.
10. Enjoy your Cinnamon Pear Sauce!

Key Chapter 4 Takeaways

- Most ingredients in desserts cannot be canned including nuts, dairy, and grains.
- There are several healthy alternatives to the sugar commonly found in most water bath canning recipes.
- Blueberries make a wonderful dessert option because not only are they sweet in taste but they can also prevent heart disease.
- Tart apples such as Granny Smith make the best pie apples.
- Rhubarb has so many bountiful health benefits that Russia tried to create a monopoly on it in the 18th century.

Chapter 5
Pickles

"Good ideas, like good pickles, are crisp, enduring, and devilishly hard to make."

- Rushworth Kidder

Pickling 101

Pickling is one of the oldest forms of preservation. For centuries, people have been fermenting fruits and vegetables in brines. While the process is similar to older practices, it has evolved, so make sure to follow a recipe that aligns with the USDA's canning guidelines. Pickling gives the produce a unique flavor, different from its original taste. The most commonly pickled vegetable is a cucumber. This is what commercially sold pickles are made out of. (Though, technically, anything that has gone through the process of pickling can be called a pickle.) While the process of pickling isn't difficult, it does take a while. Home canners who are just starting out can easily accomplish pickling as long as they have the time.

There are a couple of ways to successfully pickle any fruit or vegetable. The fastest is the quick-pack method. This would be the best place to start for new canners. Instead of using lactic acid in fermentation, this method utilizes the acetic acid in vinegar. Most recipes will call for white distilled or cider vinegar. With either ingredient, make sure it has 5% acidity. While homemade products are usually better, not when pickling. Homemade vinegar often isn't acidic enough. If you choose the quick-pack method don't add alum as a firming agent. Alum only works when the pickles are fermented. Even with a quick-pack, the flavor of the produce takes weeks to develop. Keep this in mind when choosing a time to use your canned pickles.

The method of fermenting or brining the produce will take several weeks to cure. You will know that your product has cured once the texture and color has changed. Sodium is a very important part of fermenting, so make sure not to use reduced salt products. There are different methods to fruit and relish involving sugar. Recipes will usually call for brown or white but keep in mind brown causes a darker brine. Adding in spices can also do this. This is normal and you shouldn't be afraid to experiment with different spices to find what works best for your pickles. If you are curious about the process of sun pickles, it's not USDA approved. The yeast inside a jar sitting out in sunlight will die and ruin the fermentation of the pickles.

Like most water bath canning, there is a science to pickling. It's important to double check your ingredients and pay attention to how much of everything you need. If something is off, it can result in a less-than-ideal final product. Recipes that aren't approved by the USDA can ruin the product and you'll end up with unnecessary waste.

For the best results, only pickle fresh and firm ingredients. The best time to do this is less than 24 hours after obtaining them. Double check for spoilage before you begin working with any fruits or vegetables. The pickling process will not improve any structural or flavor quality. If you have any specific question about pickling, you can always get in contact with your local extension service.

Pickled Vegetables

Dill With It Pickles

Why not start pickling with a classic? Pickling may seem daunting at first, but just like water bath canning, you'll be pickling everything you can like a pro in no time. Every year, Americans eat nine pounds of pickles per person. With over 300 million people, that's a lot of pickles. Traditional pickles come from fermented cucumbers. Cucumbers are harvested in the summer, around 50 to 70 days after being planted. They will need a good amount of room to grow, but they're still an essential plant for any home garden.

Amount: Four pints

Ingredients: *(See page 172 for Measurement Conversion)*

- 3 lbs pickling cucumbers
- 4 teaspoons dill seeds
- 2 teaspoons mustard seeds
- 4 cloves garlic
- 16 whole black peppercorns
- 2 cups water
- 1 ½ cups white vinegar
- 2 tablespoons pickling salt
- 1 tablespoons sugar

Directions :

1. Prepare all the canning equipment. Wash the jars and sterilize them if necessary. Add water to the canner but wait to boil.
2. Cut the cucumbers into small pieces that will fit in a jar and divide them up between the pints.
3. Before adding the brine to the jar, put in a mixture of 1 teaspoon dill seeds, ½ teaspoon mustard seeds, 1 clove garlic and 4 whole peppercorns into each.

4. To make the brine, combine water, white vinegar, pickling salt and sugar into a pot. Boil over medium heat to dissolve sugar and salt.
5. Pour the brine into the jars, leaving ½ inch of space. Wipe the jar's rim and put on the lid.
6. Using a jar lifter, gently place the jars in the canner, making sure there are 1-2 inches of water above them.
7. Bring the canner to a boil and let it process for 10 minutes. Adjust time for altitude differences.
8. After the time is up, turn off the heat and remove the canner's lid. Let it stand for five minutes before removal.
9. To remove the jars, use your jar lifter and let them cool for 24 hours before checking the seal.
10. Enjoy your pickles!

In a Real Pickle Pickled Onions

Did you know that the Shakespeare play *The Tempest* coined the phrase, "in a pickle?" This was used then how we still use the phrase today, to mean being in a difficult situation. What does this have to do with onions? Not a thing, but it will come in handy for any Shakespeare trivia nights. Onions can be harvested at the end of summer or early fall. This is signaled by the leaves on the neck of the plant starting to slump over. Onions have developed a reputation as being difficult to grow at home, but with a little care and a lot of love, you can make it work.

Amount: Four half pints

Ingredients: *(See page 172 for Measurement Conversion)*

- 8 cups thinly sliced sweet onions
- 2 tablespoons canning salt
- 1 cups white vinegar
- 1 cup sugar
- 1 teaspoon dried thyme

Directions :

1. Prepare all the canning equipment. Wash the jars and sterilize them if necessary. Add water to the canner but wait to boil.
2. In a colander, sprinkle salt over your prepared onions and toss to ensure coverage. Let stand for one hour before washing and draining the onions.
3. In a Dutch oven, combine vinegar, sugar, and thyme. Bring the mixture to a boil.
4. Add onions and return to a boil. Then let simmer, uncovered, for 10 minutes.
5. Funnel the brine into the jar, leaving ½ inch of space. Wipe the jar's rim and put on the lid.
6. Using a jar lifter, gently place the jars in the canner, making sure there are 1-2 inches of water above them.
7. Bring the canner to a boil and let it process for 10 minutes. Adjust time for altitude differences.

8. After the time is up, turn off the heat and remove the canner's lid. Let it stand for five minutes before removal.
9. To remove the jars, use your jar lifter and let them cool for 24 hours before checking the seal.
10. Enjoy your pickled onions!

Rise and Brine Pickled Vegetable Mix

Fun pickle fact #3—In 2000, the Philadelphia Eagles attributed drinking pickle juice to their enormous win against the Cowboys. While pickle juice is healthy for you, I don't think it endows football players with amazing game-winning abilities. I could be wrong, though. Now imagine what powers the brine of all these vegetables combined could do. With an ingredient list as big as this, it's important to invest in as many fresh veggies as possible. Especially if you have a match coming up.

Amount: Six pints

Ingredients: *(See page 172 for Measurement Conversion)*

- 2 ears of corn
- 3 cups cauliflower florets
- 3 medium red sweet peppers, seeded and cut into 1-inch pieces
- 12 ounces green beans, trimmed and cut into 1-inch pieces
- 3 medium carrots, cut into 1/2-inch slices
- 2 medium onions, cut into small wedges
- 3 cups water

- 3 cups white vinegar
- 1 cup sugar
- 1 tablespoon kosher salt
- 18 cloves garlic, smashed
- 1 ½ teaspoons crushed red pepper

Directions:

1. Prepare all the canning equipment and prepare corn by husking it and cutting the cobs into small 1-inch pieces. Wash the jars and sterilize them if necessary. Add water to the canner but wait to boil.
2. In a large pot, combine the corn, cauliflower, sweet peppers, green beans, carrots, onions with enough water to cover it. Bring vegetables to boiling. Cook, uncovered, for three minutes
3. Remove the vegetables from the heat and drain them before packing them into the jars.
4. Add cloves and crushed pepper to each jar.
5. In another pot combine the water, vinegar, sugar, and salt to make the brine. Bring this mixture to boiling and stir to dissolve sugar.
6. Funnel the brine into the jars, leaving ½ inch of space. Wipe the jar's rim and put on the lid.
7. Using a jar lifter, gently place the jars in the canner, making sure there are 1-2 inches of water above them.
8. Bring the canner to a boil and let it process for 10 minutes. Adjust time for altitude differences. After the time is up, turn off the heat

and remove the canner's lid. Let it stand for five minutes before removal.
9. To remove the jars, use your jar lifter and let them cool for 24 hours before checking the seal.
10. Enjoy your pickled vegetable mix!

Pickled Fruit

Perfect Pickled Peaches

Veggies aren't the only thing that can be pickled. Pickled peaches result in a tangy, sweet but sour, and very unique taste. Peaches are probably one of the most popular fruits to be pickled. My favorite way to use pickled peaches is to pair them with roasted pork or a salad for a lighter option. If you're curious about peaches and the harvest times, I have provided the information in Chapter 3 under the recipe Peachy Keen Chutney.

Amount: Four quarts

Ingredients: *(See page 172 for Measurement Conversion)*

- 4 pounds peaches, blanched and peeled
- 4 cups sugar
- 1 cup white vinegar
- 1 cup water
- 2 tablespoons cloves, whole
- 5 cinnamon sticks

Directions:

1. Prepare all the canning equipment. Wash the jars and sterilize them if necessary. Add water to the canner but wait to boil.
2. In a large pot, combine the sugar, vinegar, and water. Bring the mixture to a boil for five minutes.
3. Press one or two cloves into each peach before adding them to the pot.
4. Boil for 20 minutes, or until peaches are tender.
5. Spoon in the peaches and then funnel the brine into the jars, leaving ½ inch of space. Wipe the jar's rim and put on the lid.

6. Using a jar lifter, gently place the jars in the canner, making sure there are 1-2 inches of water above them.
7. Bring the canner to a boil and let it process for 10 minutes. Adjust time for altitude differences.
8. After the time is up, turn off the heat and remove the canner's lid. Let it stand for five minutes before removal.
9. To remove the jars, use your jar lifter and let them cool for 24 hours before checking the seal.
10. Enjoy your pickled peaches!

Picturesque Pickled Apricots

Another great fruit to pickle is apricots. Apricots and peaches are similar fruits, but they do have different tastes. Apricots tend to be more tart than the sweet peach. Harvest season for apricots begins at the end of summer. They are mostly grown in California due the sunny weather conditions. Growing your own apricot tree is possible anywhere in the United States, just make sure you provide the right soil.

Amount: Five half pints

Ingredients: *(See page 172 for Measurement Conversion)*

- 2 pounds ripe apricots
- 1 cup white balsamic vinegar
- ½ cup sweet vermouth
- ½ cup honey

- ½ cup water
- 2, 3-inch sticks cinnamon, broken
- 6 whole cloves

Directions:

1. Prepare all the canning equipment. Wash the jars and sterilize them if necessary. Add water to the canner but wait to boil.
2. In a saucepan, combine the vinegar, vermouth, honey, water, cinnamon, and cloves. Bring mixture to boiling before letting it simmer, uncovered, for five minutes.
3. Remove from the heat source and let it stand for 30 minutes. Remove and discard cinnamon and cloves from mixture.
4. In a different large saucepan, blanch the apricots before removing skins.
5. To prepare the apricots for going into the jars, Cut quarters and remove pits.
6. Back to the syrup mixture. Return it to a boil.
7. Funnel the syrup into a heated jar, leaving ½ inch of space. Wipe the jar's rim and put on the lid. Using a jar lifter, gently place the jars in the canner, making sure there are 1-2 inches of water above them.
8. Bring the canner to a boil and let it process for 10 minutes. Adjust time for altitude differences. After the time is up, turn off the heat

and remove the canner's lid. Let it stand for five minutes before removal.

9. To remove the jars, use your jar lifter and let them cool for 24 hours before checking the seal.
10. Enjoy your pickled apricots!

Popular Pickled Fruit Cocktail

You can pickle really any fruit, as demonstrated in the recipe below. Just make sure to choose a combination that complement each other. This might take some time through trial and error. Some of my favorite ingredients to use are cherries, strawberries, and peaches. Make sure to research the process of pickling whichever fruit you choose to make sure you have the proper way to process them.

Amount: Three pints

Ingredients: *(See page 172 for Measurement Conversion)*

- 2 cups of fresh fruit
- 1 cup vinegar
- 1 cup water
- ½ cup sugar
- 1 tablespoons salt
- Add any spice or herb to flavor

Directions:

1. Prepare all the canning equipment. Wash the jars and sterilize them if necessary. Add water to the canner but wait to boil.
2. Prep the fruit by washing and cutting it.
3. Divide the fruit evenly between jars.
4. In a saucepan, combine the vinegar, sugar, water, and salt. Bring the mixture to boiling before letting it simmer, uncovered, for five minutes.
5. Funnel the brine into a heated jar, leaving 1/2 inch of space. Add spices and herbs to top it off.
6. Wipe the jar's rim and put on the lid. Using a jar lifter, gently place the jars in the canner, making sure there are 1-2 inches of water above them.
7. Bring the canner to a boil and let it process for 20 minutes. Adjust time for altitude differences.
8. After the time is up, turn off the heat and remove the canner's lid. Let it stand for five minutes before removal.
9. To remove the jars, use your jar lifter and let them cool for 24 hours before checking the seal.
10. Enjoy your pickled fruit cocktail!

Relish

Relished Dill Pickled Relish

Despite the fact that people have been pickling for centuries, relish has only been around since the 19th century. Relish, like pickles, doesn't have to be made from just cucumbers. You can make relish from just about any fruit or vegetable. That said, I have ignored this fact and have only compiled cucumber-based recipes. Don't worry, they are all still delicious and unique. It may be basic, but there's a reason why dill is so popular. This recipe makes for the perfect addition to any cookout. The trick to any relish recipe is mastering your herbs and spices.

Amount: Seven pints

Ingredients: *(See page 172 for Measurement Conversion)*

- 9 pounds pickling cucumber
- ½ cup pickling salt
- 2 teaspoons turmeric
- 4 cup water
- 3 cups white vinegar
- 1 cup apple cider vinegar
- 1 ½ cups white onion, diced
- 1 tablespoons sugar
- 2 tablespoons dill seed
- ¼ cup red pepper

Directions:

1. Wash, cut, and deseed the cucumbers. Pulse them in a food processor to get desired size. Dice the onion and pepper as well.
2. Prepare all the canning equipment. Wash the jars and sterilize them if necessary. Add water to the canner but wait to boil.
3. Put the cucumber in a bowl and sprinkle it with salt and turmeric before adding the water. Let sit for two hours uncovered. Afterwards drain the cucumbers.
4. In a saucepan, mix the cucumber with onion, pepper, sugar, and dill seed. Pour both vinegars over the mixture before bringing it to a boil.
5. Funnel the relish into the jar, leaving ¼ inch of space. Wipe the jar's rim and put on the lid.
6. Using a jar lifter, gently place the jars in the canner, making sure there are 1-2 inches of water above them.
7. Bring the canner to a boil and let it process for 15 minutes. Adjust time for altitude differences.
8. After the time is up, turn off the heat and remove the canner's lid. Let it stand for five minutes before removal.
9. To remove the jars, use your jar lifter and let them cool for 24 hours before checking the seal.
10. Enjoy your dill pickled relish!

Relished Sweet Pickled Relish

Sweet pickled relish is another classic version of cucumber-based relish. The big difference between the two is the taste. Dill is more savory while sweet relish is, you guessed it, sweet. If you are having a hard time choosing between the two then you're outta luck. Both are healthy, delicious, and go well with hot dogs. It's all about personal flavor, and personally, I like both flavors. It's a good choice to can both and let your food mood decide what you want to eat that day. It is better to be prepared than disappointed when it comes to relish.

Amount: Four pints

Ingredients: *(See page 172 for Measurement Conversion)*

- 4 cups finely chopped cucumbers
- 2 cups finely chopped sweet peppers red or yellow
- 2 cups finely chopped onion
- ¼ cup kosher salt
- 3 ½ cups sugar
- 2 cups cider vinegar
- 1 tablespoon mustard seed
- 1 tablespoon celery seed

Directions:

1. In a food processor, chop up onion, pepper, and cucumber. Measure out what you need before placing it all in a bowl.
2. Stir in salt before covering it with ice water and setting it aside for two hours.
3. Prepare all the canning equipment. Wash the jars and sterilize them if necessary. Add water to the canner but wait to boil.
4. In a large stock pot, combine sugar, vinegar, celery seed, and mustard seed. Bring mixture to a boil.
5. Stir in drained vegetables and let simmer for 10 minutes.
6. Funnel the relish into a heated jar, leaving ¼ inch of space. Wipe the jar's rim and put on the lid. Using a jar lifter, gently place the jars in the canner, making sure there are 1-2 inches of water above them.
7. Bring the canner to a boil and let it process for 15 minutes. Adjust time for altitude differences.
8. After the time is up, turn off the heat and remove the canner's lid. Let it stand for five minutes before removal.
9. To remove the jars, use your jar lifter and let them cool for 24 hours before checking the seal.
10. Enjoy your sweet pickled relish!

Relished Jalapeno Relish

For the finale to this cucumber-based relish trilogy I offer a spicy alternative to the previous two recipes. This relish is made with the addition of jalapenos. This pepper brings a perfect amount of heat to one of the world's most favorite condiments. Jalapenos are similar to the chili pepper, but tend to be hotter in flavor. They are commercially grown in relatively the same places though, such as Texas and New Mexico. This spicy pepper makes for a great garden vegetable as well. Jalapenos take 90 days to grow to full size. Harvesting should usually take place around June.

Amount: Seven pints

Ingredients: *(See page 172 for Measurement Conversion)*

- 1 1/2 quarts jalapenos, finely chopped
- 1 quart cucumber, finely chopped
- 2 large onions, finely chopped
- 1/4 cup salt
- 5 1/4 cups sugar
- 3 cups cider vinegar
- 4 teaspoons pickling spices

Directions:

1. In a large bowl, combine jalapenos, cucumbers, onions, and salt. Cover the mixture with cold water and let it stand for two hours.
2. Prepare all the canning equipment. Wash the jars and sterilize them if necessary. Add water to the canner but wait to boil.
3. In a large pot, combine the sugar and vinegar. Use a cheesecloth to add in the spices.

4. Bring to a boil and simmer for 15 minute.

5. Add in the vegetables and let simmer for another 10 minutes before removing the cheesecloth.

6. Funnel the relish into a heated jar, leaving ¼ inch of space. Wipe the jar's rim and put on the lid.

7. Using a jar lifter, gently place the jars in the canner, making sure there are 1-2 inches of water above them.

8. Bring the canner to a boil and let it process for 10 minutes. Adjust time for altitude differences. After the time is up, turn off the heat and remove the canner's lid. Let it stand for five minutes before removal.

9. To remove the jars, use your jar lifter and let them cool for 24 hours before checking the seal.

10. Enjoy your jalapeno relish!

Key Chapter 5 Takeaways

- The art of pickling had been around for centuries.
- There are a couple ways to pickle your produce, like quick-packing or fermentation.
- Pickling vegetables is an easy way to raise the acidity so they can be processed in a water bath canner.
- Vegetables aren't the only thing that can be pickled; fruit makes for great pickled treats are well.

Chapter 6
Tomatoes

"Canned tomatoes are like summer saved all that deep sun-kissed flavor ready to be enjoyed."

- Better Homes and Gardens

Tomato Recipes

Dice to Meet You Diced Tomatoes

Everyone knows by now that tomatoes are a fruit. Well, at least everyone else but Americans. For custom regulations, the U.S. supreme court ruled tomatoes as a vegetable. I'm not a politician, but I can tell you tomatoes have seeds and are by all definitions a fruit. To be fair, they probably wouldn't taste good in a fruit salad. On the other side of the coin, who are we to make judgements when we are only the second largest producer in the world. China takes the number one spot. Tomatoes are usually ready to be harvested around 60 to 85 days after planting them. This is usually done in the summer for the best results.

Amount: Nine pints

Ingredients: *(See page 172 for Measurement Conversion)*

- 9 pounds tomatoes
- 9 tablespoons bottled lemon juice

Directions:

1. Prepare all the canning equipment. Wash the jars and sterilize them if necessary. Add water to the canner but wait to boil.
2. Blanch tomatoes and remove skin. Then core and dice them as well. Save any excess of juice
3. Add a teaspoon of lemon juice to the bottom of each jar.
4. Funnel the tomatoes into a heated jar, leaving 1/2 inch of space. Press in the tomatoes with a spoon to release juices. If needed add more juice to fill the jar.
5. Wipe the jar's rim and put on the lid.
6. Using a jar lifter, gently place the jars in the canner, making sure there are 1-2 inches of water above them.
7. Bring the canner to a boil and let it process for 85 minutes. Adjust time for altitude differences.
8. After the time is up, turn off the heat and remove the canner's lid. Let it stand for five minutes before removal.
9. To remove the jars, use your jar lifter and let them cool for 24 hours before checking the seal.
10. Enjoy your diced tomatoes!

Cherished Cherry Tomatoes

Cherry tomatoes, in layman terms, are just tiny tomatoes. They are a great source of vitamin A, C, and E, and are often considered a superfood. While cherry tomatoes make for a healthy snack raw, they can also be canned whole. Since they are so small, the process is similar to how you would can a berry. When it comes to choosing between cherry tomatoes and regular-sized tomatoes, it doesn't matter. Their nutritional value is pretty much the same. Despite their name, cherry tomatoes can come in a variety of colors such as orange, purple, or yellow.

Amount: Four pints

Ingredients: *(See page 172 for Measurement Conversion)*

- 10 cups cherry tomatoes
- 1 tablespoon bottled lemon juice
- 1 teaspoon salt

Directions:

1. Prepare all the canning equipment. Wash the jars and sterilize them if necessary. Add water to the canner but wait to boil.
2. In a pan mix the tomatoes with a little bit of water. For five cups of tomatoes, add one cup of water.
3. On medium-high, bring the tomatoes to a boil. Let boil for five minutes.
4. Funnel the cherry tomatoes into a heated jar, leaving 1/2 inch of space.
5. Add salt and lemon juice to each jar.
6. Wipe the jar's rim and put on the lid. Using a jar lifter, gently place the jars in the canner, making sure there are 1-2 inches of water above them.
7. Bring the canner to a boil and let it process for 35 minutes. Adjust time for altitude differences.
8. After the time is up, turn off the heat and remove the canner's lid. Let it stand for five minutes before removal.
9. To remove the jars, use your jar lifter and let them cool for 24 hours before checking the seal.
10. Enjoy your cherry tomatoes!

Whole Lotta Whole Tomato

It can not be more simple to can whole tomatoes. While you can't actually can a whole tomato, mostly because it wouldn't fit, you can can them in large halves. Fun fact about tomatoes, more than 600,000 seeds were sent up to outer space. The seeds weren't grown out there, but they did spend time on the international space station before being grown back on earth for an experiment. That is quite an amazing feat for a fruit that's lying about being a vegetable. The good news is that if space tomato seeds can grow, so can normal ones in your own garden.

Amount: Nine pints

Ingredients: *(See page 172 for Measurement Conversion)*

- 13 pounds Roma tomatoes
- 9 tablespoons. concentrated lemon juice.

Directions:

- Prepare all the canning equipment. Wash the jars and sterilize them if necessary. Add water to the canner but wait to boil.
- Blanch tomatoes and remove skin. Save any juices.
- Add a teaspoon of lemon juice to the bottom of each jar.
- Funnel the tomatoes into a heated jar, leaving ½ inch of space. You may need to cut the tomatoes into large but smaller pieces.
- Wipe the jar's rim and put on the lid.

- Using a jar lifter, gently place the jars in the canner, making sure there are 1-2 inches of water above them.

- Bring the canner to a boil and let it process for 85 minutes. Adjust time for altitude differences.

- After the time is up, turn off the heat, and remove the canner's lid. Let it stand for five minutes before removal.

- To remove the jars, use your jar lifter and let them cool for 24 hours before checking the seal.

- Enjoy your whole tomatoes!

Salsa Recipes

Mild Salsa

Whether you're using it as a dip for corn chips or to spice up your tortilla, Taco Tuesday is not complete without salsa. This recipe provides a mild version to the Mexican-American food staple we're used to. There are many ways to make salsa and when it comes to your canning pantry, I suggest having a variety of types. Mild salsa is one of the easiest salsas to make, but to prevent canning fatigue, you'll want more flavors, especially if you're canning months ahead. Follow this recipe and the next two below for a fuller canning pantry.

Amount: Nine pints

Ingredients: *(See page 172 for Measurement Conversion)*

- 10 cups tomatoes, peeled and cored
- 6 cups diced peppers, mixture of mild and hot
- 4 cups chopped onions (about 6 medium onions)
- 3 cloves garlic, peeled
- 2 tablespoons cilantro, finely chopped
- 1 tablespoon salt
- ½ teaspoon black pepper
- 1 cup white vinegar

Directions:

1. Prepare all the canning equipment. Wash the jars and sterilize them if necessary. Add water to the canner but wait to boil.

2. Blanch the tomatoes to remove skin. Then squeeze the juice and pulp out.
3. Dice the tomatoes. Remove seeds from the peppers before chopping them up and chop up the onion and garlic in a food processor.
4. In a large pot add the tomatoes, the pepper, the onions, garlic, cilantro, salt, pepper, and vinegar.
5. On medium-high heat bring mixture to a boil then simmer for 15 minutes,
6. Funnel the salsa into a heated jar, leaving ½ inch of space. Wipe the jar's rim and put on the lid. Using a jar lifter, gently place the jars in the canner, making sure there are 1-2 inches of water above them.
7. Bring the canner to a boil and let it process for 15 minutes. Adjust time for altitude differences.
8. After the time is up, turn off the heat and remove the canner's lid. Let it stand for five minutes before removal.
9. To remove the jars, use your jar lifter and let them cool for 24 hours before checking the seal.
10. Enjoy your mild salsa!

Spicy Salsa

Spicy salsa is a great way to use up any leftover peppers from your garden. Even if you don't have a garden, it is still worth the time to make this great salsa for Taco Tuesday. The secret to this salsa's success is the diversity of produce. You'll need two different types of bell peppers, three different types of peppers in total, and two different types of tomatoes. With the addition of onion, that might seem like a lot, but it actually produces a wonderful cacophony of flavor. For more information on the hot pepper, check out Chapter 7's hot sauce recipe.

Amount: Seven pints

Ingredients: *(See page 172 for Measurement Conversion)*

- 5 lbs tomatoes, ½ regular, ½ Romas
- 2 lbs peppers, mix of red and green bell peppers with 6 hot peppers
- 1 lb white onions, diced
- 5 cloves garlic
- 1 cup apple cider vinegar
- 2 teaspoons ground cumin
- 1 ½ teaspoons chili powder
- 2 ½ teaspoons espresso powder
- ½ teaspoon ground black pepper
- 3 teaspoons kosher salt
- 1/2 cup chopped fresh cilantro

Directions:

1. Prepare all the canning equipment. Wash the jars and sterilize them if necessary. Add water to the canner but wait to boil.

2. In an oven, broil the tomatoes and peppers until the skin is visibly blistering. Flip and roast the other side. Remove stems and core but keep the skin.
3. In a blender, blend the roasted tomatoes, all the juices from the pan, garlic, and ½ of the diced onions until smooth.
4. In a saucepan, add all the ingredients, including the diced peppers and remaining diced onions, and bring to a boil. Simmer for 10 minutes, stirring occasionally.
5. Funnel the salsa into a heated jar, leaving ½ inch of space. Wipe the jar's rim and put on the lid.
6. Using a jar lifter, gently place the jars in the canner, making sure there are 1-2 inches of water above them.
7. Bring the canner to a boil and let it process for 15minutes. Adjust time for altitude differences.
8. After the time is up, turn off the heat and remove the canner's lid. Let it stand for five minutes before removal.
9. To remove the jars, use your jar lifter and let them cool for 24 hours before checking the seal.
10. Enjoy your spicy salsa!

Salsa Verde

Salsa Verde is made with tomatillos. In Spanish this translates to "little tomatoes," but tomatillos aren't little tomatoes. To further complicate their identity crisis, they are also referred to as "husk tomatoes." They are pretty similar and are considered fruits for the same reason tomatoes are but they have different flavors. Tomatillos have to be husked like corn does, but they grow on stems like a tomato instead of a stalk. For the most part, this peculiar plant is grown in Mexico, but places in the United States like Texas and New Mexico have had success planting them. Tomatillos are harvested in the morning hours during midsummer to fall.

Amount: Five half pints

Ingredients: *(See page 172 for Measurement Conversion)*

- 5 ½ cups tomatillos, chopped husked and cored
- 1 cup chopped onion
- 1 cup peppers, chopped, mix of green bell, jalapenos, and Thai chili
- 6 cloves garlic, minced
- ⅓ cup cilantro, minced
- 1 tablespoon cumin
- 1 teaspoon paprika
- 1 ½ teaspoons salt
- ½ cup white vinegar
- 3 tablespoons lime juice

Directions:

1. Prepare all the canning equipment. Wash the jars and sterilize them if necessary. Add water to the canner but wait to boil.
2. Preheat the oven to 500 °F. On a baking sheet place ¾ of your tomatillos and roast for 20 minutes.

3. Chop up onions and pepper in a food processor.
4. Remove hot tomatillo and let them cool before pulsing through the food processor with the remaining ¼ of raw tomatillos.
5. In a saucepan, add onions, peppers, tomatillos, garlic, cumin, paprika, salt, vinegar, and lime juice. Bring mixture to a boil and then let simmer for 12 minutes.
6. Funnel the salsa into a heated jar, leaving ½ inch of space. Wipe the jar's rim and put on the lid.
7. Using a jar lifter, gently place the jars in the canner, making sure there are 1-2 inches of water above them.
8. Bring the canner to a boil and let it process for 15 minutes. Adjust time for altitude differences. After the time is up, turn off the heat and remove the canner's lid. Let it stand for five minutes before removal.
9. To remove the jars, use your jar lifter and let them cool for 24 hours before checking the seal.
10. Enjoy your salsa verde!

Tomato Sauce Recipes

Pasta La Vista, Baby Sauce

Before you start making tomato-based sauces, it's important to know pasta sauce is technically not the same thing as marinara sauce. Pasta sauce has meat or vegetables in it, while marinara typically doesn't. Water bath canners cannot can meat or vegetables. That can only be done in a pressure canner. Below I've provided a recipe to the base of the pasta sauce. Meat or vegetables can be added to the actual food when the jar's contents are ready to be eaten. Okay, maybe it's not that important to know pasta sauce isn't marinara sauce because the technicalities have no bearing on the recipe below.

Amount: Nine quarts

Ingredients: *(See page 172 for Measurement Conversion)*

- 25 pounds tomatoes
- 4 large green peppers
- 4 large onions, cut
- 24 ounces tomato paste
- 1/4 cup canola oil
- 2/3 cup sugar
- 1/4 cup salt
- 8 garlic cloves, minced
- 2 teaspoons dried parsley flakes

- 2 teaspoons dried basil
- 2 teaspoons crushed red pepper flake
- 2 teaspoons Worcestershire sauce
- 2 bay leaves
- 1 cup 2 tablespoons bottled lemon juice

Directions:

1. Prepare all the canning equipment. Wash the jars and sterilize them if necessary. Add water to the canner but wait to boil.
2. Blanch the tomatoes before peeling and quartering them.
3. In a food processor, pulse green peppers and onions until finely chopped.
4. In a stockpot, mix in all ingredients except lemon juice. Cover with water and bring to a boil. Then let simmer, for 4-5 hours uncovered, stirring occasionally.
5. Add 2 tablespoons lemon juice to each jar.
6. Funnel the sauce into a heated jar, leaving ½ inch of space. Wipe the jar's rim and put on the lid. Using a jar lifter, gently place the jars in the canner, making sure there are 1-2 inches of water above them.
7. Bring the canner to a boil and let it process for 40 minutes. Adjust time for altitude differences.
8. After the time is up, turn off the heat and remove the canner's lid. Let it stand for five minutes before removal.

9. To remove the jars, use your jar lifter and let them cool for 24 hours before checking the seal.
10. Enjoy your pasta sauce!

Marinara Sauce

If you liked the last recipe name and were disappointed to find this is just called marinara sauce, I'm sorry, but I've peaked when it comes to tomato-sauce-related puns. So what's the difference between canning pasta sauce and marinara sauce? Time mostly. It's just a simpler version of tomato sauce than pasta is. Marinara is commonly used as a dipping sauce and doesn't need to shine as much as pasta sauce does. Don't worry, if you use marinara sauce as pasta sauce it's not going to rip a hole in the time-space continuum. Marinara sauce is often used as pasta sauce even though technically they are not the same thing. In conclusion, when it comes to your pasta, do whatever you want.

Amount: Nine quarts

Ingredients: *(See page 172 for Measurement Conversion)*

- 12 pounds tomatoes
- ½ cup minced onion
- 6 cloves garlic, minced
- ¼ cup extra virgin olive oil
- 3 tablespoons brown sugar

- 2 tablespoons sea salt
- 1 tablespoon dark balsamic vinegar
- 1 ½ teaspoons dried rosemary
- 1 ½ teaspoons dried oregano
- 1 ½ teaspoons dried basil
- 1 ½ teaspoons dried thyme
- 1 teaspoon crushed fennel seeds
- ½ teaspoon dried ground sage
- ½ teaspoon freshly ground black pepper
- 2 bay leaves
- 1 tablespoon lemon juice

Directions:

1. Prepare all the canning equipment. Wash the jars and sterilize them if necessary. Add water to the canner but wait to boil.
2. Blanch the tomatoes before peeling and squeezing out the seeds. Chop up the tomatoes.
3. In a large pot, mix in all the ingredients except lemon juice. Bring to a boil. Then let simmer, for two hours uncovered, stirring occasionally.
4. In an immersion blender, puree the mariner to a desired consistency
5. Add 2 tablespoons lemon juice to each jar.

6. Funnel the sauce into a heated jar, leaving ½ inch of space. Wipe the jar's rim and put on the lid.
7. Using a jar lifter, gently place the jars in the canner, making sure there are 1-2 inches of water above them.
8. Bring the canner to a boil and let it process for 40 minutes. Adjust time for altitude differences. After the time is up, turn off the heat and remove the canner's lid. Let it stand for five minutes before removal.
9. To remove the jars, use your jar lifter and let them cool for 24 hours before checking the seal.
10. Enjoy your marinara sauce!

Pizza Sauce

Wait a minute, isn't pizza sauce just marinara sauce which is pasta sauce without the meat? No, it's slightly different. Pizza sauce needs to spread gracefully across the crust. Marinara is too chunky to achieve this. While the ingredients are similar and the taste has a minute difference, they are made with different methods. Could you put marinara on a pizza? Probably, but it won't spread as nicely. Does this small difference in texture really deserve a different name though? It's not up to us, it's up to the tomato gods and they have spoken. Pasta sauce goes on pasta, marinara is a dip, and pizza sauce goes on pizza.

Amount: Seven pints

Ingredients: *(See page 172 for Measurement Conversion)*

- 22 pounds tomatoes
- 3 cups onions, chopped
- 6 cloves garlic, minced
- ¼ cups olive oil
- 2 tablespoons dried basil
- 1 tablespoon dried oregano
- 1 tablespoon dried thyme
- ½ tablespoon black pepper
- 1 tablespoon sugar or honey
- 2 tablespoons salt
- 1 teaspoon crushed red pepper flakes
- 1 tablespoon lemon juice

Directions:

1. Wash, core, and halve tomatoes. Then, in a stockpot, bring the tomatoes to a boil. Strain to remove seeds and peels.
2. Prepare all the canning equipment. Wash the jars and sterilize them if necessary. Add water to the canner but wait to boil.
3. In a larger stockpot, cook onions and garlic in olive oil over medium heat for 5-10 minutes.
4. Add tomato puree and all the seasonings before bringing mixture to a boil. Reduce heat and cook for about 30 minutes, uncovered.
5. Process with an immersion blender to make a smoother sauce
6. Bring back to a boil; reduce heat and simmer, uncovered, for one hour. Stir occasionally.

7. Funnel the sauce into a heated jar, leaving ½ inch of space. Wipe the jar's rim and put on the lid. Using a jar lifter, gently place the jars in the canner, making sure there are 1-2 inches of water above them.
8. Bring the canner to a boil and let it process for 35 minutes. Adjust time for altitude differences. After the time is up, turn off the heat and remove the canner's lid. Let it stand for five minutes before removal.
9. To remove the jars, use your jar lifter and let them cool for 24 hours before checking the seal.
10. Enjoy your pizza sauce!

Tomato Juice Recipes

Tomato Juice

There are a million uses for tomato juice. You can drink it, you can add it to a cocktail, and you can even use it to get the smell of skunk off of you. Tomato juice is very rich in nutrients and provides several important vitamins. Like blueberries, it can also be a source of antioxidants. Store-bought tomato sauce can be full of unnecessary sugar and salt, so the best way to take advantage of the nutritional value of tomato sauce is to make your own at home. The recipe below is a quick way to turn any garden yields into a tasty and healthy drink.

Amount: Six pint jars

Ingredients: *(See page 172 for Measurement Conversion)*

- 1 bushel of tomatoes. half Roma and half regular
- 15 teaspoons salt

Directions :

1. Prepare all the canning equipment. Wash the jars and sterilize them if necessary. Add water to the canner but wait to boil.
2. Core and peel tomatoes.
3. Place a few of the tomatoes in a large stock pot and squish them with a potato masher. Add the rest of the tomatoes while bringing the pot to a boil.
4. Put the mixture through a food mill and discard the pulp. Put the juice back in the stock pot.
5. Bring to a full rolling boil.
6. Add salt.
7. Funnel the juice into a heated jar, leaving ½ inch of space. Wipe the jar's rim and put on the lid. Using a jar lifter, gently place the jars in the canner, making sure there are 1-2 inches of water above them.
8. Bring the canner to a boil and let it process for 25 minutes. Adjust time for altitude differences. After the time is up, turn off the heat

and remove the canner's lid. Let it stand for five minutes before removal.
9. To remove the jars, use your jar lifter and let them cool for 24 hours before checking the seal.
10. Enjoy your tomato juice!

Fresh From the Garden Vegetable Juice

The magic of the tomato and lemon juice is that they make low-acid vegetables water bath canner friendly. Usually with some of the vegetables listed below you would use a pressure canner, which is a lot more maintenance than a water bath canner. Garden vegetable juice is a great way to use up your extra veggies without all the effort. My favorite part, as the name implies, is that you can get all the ingredients from a home garden. As someone who likes to limit their waste as much as possible, this is one of the easiest yet tastiest ways to can up extra produce.

Amount: Seven quart jars

Ingredients: *(See page 172 for Measurement Conversion)*

- 22 lbs tomatoes
- ¾ cup celery, diced
- ¾ cup bell pepper, seeded, diced
- ¾ cup carrot, peeled, diced
- ½ cup onion, peeled, diced
- ¼ cup parsley, chopped

- 1 tablespoon salt
- lemon juice

Directions:

1. Prepare all the canning equipment. Wash the jars and sterilize them if necessary. Add water to the canner but wait to boil.
2. In a large pot, mix everything but the salt and lemon juice. let it simmer for 20 minutes.
3. Put the mixture through a food mill before putting it back in the pot.
4. Add salt and reheat but don't boil the mixture.
5. Funnel the juice into a heated jar, leaving ½ inch of space. Wipe the jar's rim and put on the lid.
6. Using a jar lifter, gently place the jars in the canner, making sure there are 1-2 inches of water above them.
7. Bring the canner to a boil and let it process for 40 minutes. Adjust time for altitude differences.
8. After the time is up, turn off the heat and remove the canner's lid. Let it stand for five minutes before removal.
9. To remove the jars, use your jar lifter and let them cool for 24 hours before checking the seal.
10. Enjoy your garden vegetable juice!

Bloody Mary

This recipe is not the actual alcoholic drink. It is the mix to make the alcoholic drink. After you're done canning you can decide for yourself if you'd like to upgrade to a more adult option by adding vodka or to keep it virgin. This iconic cocktail is only 100 years old. It's believed to have been created by a Parisian bartender in the early 1920s. It was a great way to start off the roaring '20s. Before the invention of the Bloody Mary, a similar mixture to the one below was actually used to cure hangovers. Whichever way you choose to use it, it will make a delightful addition to any brunch.

Amount: Six pint jars

Ingredients: *(See page 172 for Measurement Conversion)*

- 30 pc. medium tomatoes, quartered
- 1 ½ cups green peppers, chopped
- 1 cup carrots, diced
- ½ cup celery, diced
- 1 pc. small onions, diced
- 2-3 pc. garlic cloves, minced
- ¼ cup parsley, minced
- ¼ cup sugar
- ¼ cup lemon juice
- 1 1/2 tablespoon salt
- 1 tablespoon Worcestershire sauce
- ¼ cup medium jalapeno, diced including seeds

Directions:

1. Prepare all the canning equipment. Wash the jars and sterilize them if necessary. Add water to the canner but wait to boil.
2. In a large Dutch oven, cook the tomatoes, green peppers, carrots, celery, onion, garlic, parsley, and hot peppers for 30-45 minutes.
3. After this, blend the mixture in an immersion blender until smooth.
4. Place the mixture back in the pot and add the sugar, lemon juice, Worcestershire sauce, and salt. Bring to a boil over medium, stirring frequently.

5. Funnel the mix into a heated jar, leaving ½ inch of space. Wipe the jar's rim and put on the lid.
6. Using a jar lifter, gently place the jars in the canner, making sure there are 1-2 inches of water above them.
7. Bring the canner to a boil and let it process for 40 minutes. Adjust time for altitude differences.
8. After the time is up, turn off the heat and remove the canner's lid. Let it stand for five minutes before removal.
9. To remove the jars, use your jar lifter and let them cool for 24 hours before checking the seal.
10. Enjoy your Bloody Mary!

Key Chapter 6 Takeaways

- From sauces to alcoholic beverages, there's a lot you can do with tomatoes.
- Different-sized cuts of tomatoes need different cooking times to properly be processed.
- Tomatoes are a fruit and not a vegetable due to their high acidity and ability to be canned in a water bath canner.
- Marinara sauce and pasta sauce are very similar but can still be considered two different products.
- Roma tomatoes are usually the best tomatoes to work with.

Chapter 7
Condiments

"Failure is the condiment that gives success its flavor."

-Truman Capote

Basic Condiments

Knock 'Em Out Ketchup

Ketchup is one of America's most beloved condiments. It pairs with just about any meat and is a must-have for any cookout. Just 4 tablespoons of ketchup has the same nutritional value as an entire medium-sized tomato. It was first sold in 1876 by the F. & J. Heinz company, which is still a main producer of the condiment today. Back then it was called "catsup," before the producers decided to change the name to ketchup. Since it comes from tomatoes, ketchup's taste is completely dependent on the quality of the crop. Check out Chapter 6 for more information on the harvest season.

Amount: Three pint jars

Ingredients: *(See page 172 for Measurement Conversion)*

- 4 quarts tomato puree
- 1 cup onion, chopped

- ½ cup sweet pepper, chopped
- 1 ½ cups vinegar
- 1 tablespoon canning salt
- ¼ teaspoon ground allspice
- 1 stick cinnamon
- ¾ cup sugar

Directions:

1. Prepare all the canning equipment. Wash the jars and sterilize them if necessary. Add water to the canner but wait to boil.
2. In a large pot, combine 1 quart of the tomatoes, all of the onions and sweet pepper in. Simmer until vegetables are soft.
3. Press remaining tomatoes, and the tomato mixture through a food mill to remove the seeds and skins
4. in a stockpot, bring mixture to a boil. Boil rapidly for one hour or until thickened.
5. Add vinegar, salt, sugar, cinnamon, and other seasonings.
6. Place sauce in a slow cooker on high with the cover removed until desired consistency.
7. Funnel the ketchup into a heated jar, leaving ¼ inch of space. Wipe the jar's rim and put on the lid. Using a jar lifter, gently place the jars in the canner, making sure there are 1-2 inches of water above them.

8. Bring the canner to a boil and let it process for 10 minutes. Adjust time for altitude differences. After the time is up, turn off the heat and remove the canner's lid. Let it stand for five minutes before removal.
9. To remove the jars, use your jar lifter and let them cool for 24 hours before checking the seal.
10. Enjoy your ketchup!

Better Barbecue Sauce

This American classic has been around for centuries and works as more than just a condiment. It can be used for marinating or basting pork, beef, or chicken. It's sweet but tangy flavor also makes it ideal for a topping to meat products. Many celebrity chefs have their own specific recipes, making barbecue sauce a must-have for any canning pantry. Stemming from its popularity in the south, barbecue sauce is undoubtedly one of the biggest condiments of soul food. If you're curious about any information about tomatoes or onions, check out Chapter 6, and Chapter 5's pickled onions recipe.

Amount: Six pint jars

Ingredients: *(See page 172 for Measurement Conversion)*

- 12 lbs tomato, peeled
- 3 cups onion, finely chopped
- 4 cloves garlic, chopped

- 1 ½ cups apple cider vinegar
- ½ cup bourbon
- 2 cups dark brown sugar, packed
- 1 tablespoon garlic powder
- 1 tablespoon mustard powder
- 2 tablespoons smoked paprika
- 1 teaspoon cayenne pepper
- 2 teaspoons chili flakes
- 2 tablespoons salt

Directions:

1. Prepare all the canning equipment. Wash the jars and sterilize them if necessary. Add water to the canner but wait to boil.
2. In a large stock pot, combine tomatoes, onion, and garlic and bring to a boil. Let simmer for 30 minutes.
3. Puree vegetables until smooth in the food processor.
4. Return tomato mixture to the pot and add remaining ingredients. Bring to a boil over high heat, stirring frequently. Let simmer for two hours or until mixture has thickened and darkened in color, stirring occasionally.
5. Funnel the barbecue into a heated jar, leaving ½ inch of space. Wipe the jar's rim and put on the lid.
6. Using a jar lifter, gently place the jars in the canner, making sure there are 1-2 inches of water above them.

7. Bring the canner to a boil and let it process for 20 minutes. Adjust time for altitude differences.
8. After the time is up, turn off the heat and remove the canner's lid. Let it stand for five minutes before removal.
9. To remove the jars, use your jar lifter and let them cool for 24 hours before checking the seal.
10. Enjoy your barbeque!

Marry Me Mustard

Will this recipe get you a wedding ring? Crazier things have happened, but even if you end up alone with 50 cats at least you'll have a delicious addition to your pantry. Mustard is centuries older than ketchup, first appearing in the 13th century in Dijon, France. The mustard seed comes from the mustard plant. If you're a gardener and want to try to harvest your own, the best season to grow this plant would be the spring or fall. This recipe makes a good companion to hamburgers or chicken tenders, but my personal favorite use for Marry Me Mustard is as a dip for hot pretzels.

Amount: Eight four oz jars

Ingredients: *(See page 172 for Measurement Conversion)*

- 2 cups onion, chopped
- 2 cups Pinot Grigio
- 1 cup white wine vinegar
- 1 teaspoon table salt

- 6 medium garlic cloves, coarsely chopped
- 4 whole black peppercorns
- 1 sprig fresh rosemary
- 1 cup yellow mustard seeds
- ⅓ cup dry mustard
- 2 ⅔ cups water

Directions:
1. Prepare all the canning equipment. Wash the jars and sterilize them if necessary. Add water to the canner but wait to boil.
2. In a saucepan, combine the onions, Pinot Grigio, vinegar, salt, garlic cloves, peppercorns, and rosemary and bring to a boil. Then reduce heat and let simmer for 20 minute to soften the onion.
3. Strain the mixture through a mesh strainer.
4. Add the mustard seed and dry mustard to the liquid. Cover and let sit for 24 hours at room temperature.
5. Process the mix in a blender before boiling it in a saucepan. Let simmer for 5 minutes.
6. Funnel the mustard into a heated jar, leaving ¼ inch of space. Wipe the jar's rim and put on the lid. Using a jar lifter, gently place the jars in the canner, making sure there are 1-2 inches of water above them.

7. Bring the canner to a boil and let it process for 10 minutes. Adjust time for altitude differences.

8. After the time is up, turn off the heat and remove the canner's lid. Let it stand for five minutes before removal.

9. To remove the jars, use your jar lifter and let them cool for 24 hours before checking the seal.

10. Enjoy your mustard!

Advanced Condiments

Serenading Sweet Chili Sauce

Bored of plain old ketchup or mustard? Want to try something with a little more spice? Well I got the recipe for you. This serenading sweet chili sauce is sure to kick up any meal a notch. The sweetness comes from the sugar and tomatoes but then the vinegar and peppers provide a nice contradictory sourness to the sauce. Adding a recipe like this to the pantry is a great way to avoid canning fatigue. In the traditional recipes of Thailand, sweet chili sauce is often made with hot red peppers but I've chosen a bell pepper recipe down below for a more mild taste.

Amount: Four pints

Ingredients: *(See page 172 for Measurement Conversion)*

- 16 cups small tomatoes, peeled and chopped
- 1 ¾ cups white vinegar
- 2 cups sugar
- 1 cup finely chopped onions
- 1 ½ cups finely chopped celery
- ¾ cup finely chopped bell pepper of any color
- 2 ¼ teaspoons pickling or kosher salt
- 1 ½ teaspoons ground cinnamon
- 1 ½ teaspoons ground ginger
- 1 teaspoons mustard seed

Directions:

1. Wash and chop up tomatoes and all vegetables.
2. Prepare all the canning equipment. Wash the jars and sterilize them if necessary. Add water to the canner but wait to boil.
3. In a large saucepan, combine the tomatoes, vinegar, sugar, onions, celery, bell peppers, salt, cinnamon, ginger, and mustard seeds.
4. Bring to a boil, stirring to dissolve the sugar. Let simmer for two hours, stir frequently.
5. Funnel the sauce into a heated jar, leaving ½ inch of space. Wipe the jar's rim and put on the lid.
6. Using a jar lifter, gently place the jars in the canner, making sure there are 1-2 inches of water above them.
7. Bring the canner to a boil and let it process for 15 minutes. Adjust time for altitude differences.

8. After the time is up, turn off the heat and remove the canner's lid. Let it stand for five minutes before removal.
9. To remove the jars, use your jar lifter and let them cool for 24 hours before checking the seal.
10. Enjoy your sweet chili sauce!

Horseradish Harmony

Despite its name, horseradish is not made of horses and radishes. That would not make a very good sauce. Horseradish comes from the horseradish plant. This is a root vegetable that has been grown for centuries to cultivate its medicinal properties. What makes horseradish so odd is that peak harvest season for the plant is late fall, around October or November. This would be normal if the majority of horseradish's were grown in a state with warmer weather but the horseradish capital of the world is Illinois, U.S.A.. It grows on the floodplains of the Mississippi which makes for great soil but a cold midwestern fall.

Amount: Four half pint jars

Ingredients: *(See page 172 for Measurement Conversion)*

- 1 cup sugar
- 1 tablespoon kosher salt
- 2 cups white vinegar
- 7 cups lightly packed shredded horseradish root.

Directions:

1. Prepare all the canning equipment. Wash the jars and sterilize them if necessary. Add water to the canner but wait to boil.
2. In a saucepan, combine sugar, salt and vinegar. Bring to a boil over medium high heat, stirring to dissolve sugar and salt.
3. Add horseradish and return to a boil.
4. Press down on horseradish for better immersion
5. Funnel the sauce into a heated jar, leaving ½ inch of space. Wipe the jar's rim and put on the lid.
6. Using a jar lifter, gently place the jars in the canner, making sure there are 1-2 inches of water above them.
7. Bring the canner to a boil and let it process for 10 minutes. Adjust time for altitude differences.
8. After the time is up, turn off the heat and remove the canner's lid. Let it stand for five minutes before removal.
9. To remove the jars, use your jar lifter and let them cool for 24 hours before checking the seal.
10. Enjoy your horseradish!

From the Heart Honey Mustard

I'm not sure why all the mustard names are so romantic. I suppose it's because the mustard seed has a history being an aphrodisiac. The ancient Greeks were the first to figure out the benefits it can provide to blood pressure. This is because the seeds are rich with copper, iron, magnesium and selenium. These minerals have been documented to help with blood flow. Along with this benefit, these properties have provided relief to asthma patients. So whether you are having an asthma attack or looking for a romantic meal for an anniversary this recipe will come in handy.

Amount: Two half pint jars

Ingredients: *(See page 172 for Measurement Conversion)*

- ¾ cup mustard powder
- ⅓ cup honey
- 1 cup cider vinegar
- 3 whole eggs, slightly beaten

Directions:

1. Prepare all the canning equipment. Wash the jars and sterilize them if necessary. Add water to the canner but wait to boil.
2. Place a double boiler over simmering water
3. In a double boiler, combine all the ingredients, stirring until smooth and fully mixed.
4. Cook for 10 minutes or until thick and smooth.
5. Funnel the sauce into a heated jar, leaving ½ inch of space. Wipe the jar's rim and put on the lid.
6. Using a jar lifter, gently place the jars in the canner, making sure there are 1-2 inches of water above them.
7. Bring the canner to a boil and let it process for 10 minutes. Adjust time for altitude differences.

8. After the time is up, turn off the heat and remove the canner's lid. Let it stand for five minutes before removal.
9. To remove the jars, use your jar lifter and let them cool for 24 hours before checking the seal.
10. Enjoy your honey mustard!

Dressing and Syrup Recipes

You Won't Regret this Strawberry Vinaigrette

Dressing isn't typically canned. In fact you will have difficulty finding a USDA approved recipe for any dressing. This strawberry vinaigrette is fine because it's ingredients are safe to can. Ranch dressing requires buttermilk and other dressings like French need oil. Both of these ingredients are not ideal for any canner. Another reason is that there isn't really a need for canning dressing. Most dressings can be made any time, there's no peak. There is a peak season for strawberry vinaigrette though. If you're curious about the peak seasons of strawberry check out the very first recipe in chapter 3, strawberry good jam.

Amount: Six half pint jars

Ingredients: *(See page 172 for Measurement Conversion)*

- 7 lbs strawberries

- 4 cups white vinegar
- sugar (should be equal to strawberry liquid)

Directions:

1. Put strawberries in a container and pour the vinegar over them. Cover tightly with plastic wrap and place in a 70 °F location to let stand overnight.
2. Prepare all the canning equipment. Wash the jars and sterilize them if necessary. Add water to the canner but wait to boil.
3. Strain the liquid and berries through a cheesecloth. Discard any pulp and keep clean liquid.
4. In a pot, stir in white sugar equal to the volume of liquid. Bring to a boil and immediately remove from heat.
5. Skim off any foam and discard.
6. Funnel the dressing into a heated jar, leaving ¼ inch of space. Wipe the jar's rim and put on the lid.
7. Using a jar lifter, gently place the jars in the canner, making sure there are 1-2 inches of water above them.
8. Bring the canner to a boil and let it process for 10 minutes. Adjust time for altitude differences. After the time is up, turn off the heat and remove the canner's lid. Let it stand for five minutes before removal.
9. To remove the jars, use your jar lifter and let them cool for 24 hours before checking the seal.
10. Enjoy your strawberry vinaigrette!

Seriously Good Strawberry Syrup

When it comes to regular maple syrup, the extra step of canning is actually unnecessary. Canning usually requires sugar but syrup already has a high amount in it so there's no need to add any more. When preparing syrup, it gets boiled but it's boiling point is well above that of water. When it's added to the jar, the lid just pops and it's sealed. Water bath canning will just ruin the product. What does any of this have to do with strawberry syrup? Nothing because it's a fruit byproduct and you definitely need to water bath can it. Check out the strawberry good jam recipe in chapter 3 for information on picking and growing strawberries.

Amount: Eight half pints

Ingredients: *(See page 172 for Measurement Conversion)*

- 10 cups strawberries, stemmed and crushed
- 3 cups water
- 1 strip (2-inch) lemon peel
- 2 ½ cups granulated sugar
- 3 ½ cups corn syrup
- 2 tablespoons lemon juice

Directions:

1. Prepare all the canning equipment. Wash the jars and sterilize them if necessary. Add water to the canner but wait to boil.

2. In a large pot, combine strawberries, 1½ cups of the water and the lemon peel. Boil for 5 minutes.
3. Place the mixture in a jelly bag and let it drip for at least two hours.
4. In a large pot, combine sugar and remaining 1½ cups of water.
5. Bring to a boil over medium-high heat, stirring to dissolve sugar, and cook until temperature reaches 230 °F.
6. Add strawberry juice and corn syrup. Boil for another 5 minutes, stirring occasionally. Remove from heat and add the lemon juice.
7. Funnel the syrup into a heated jar, leaving ¼ inch of space. Wipe the jar's rim and put on the lid. Using a jar lifter, gently place the jars in the canner, making sure there are 1-2 inches of water above them.
8. Bring the canner to a boil and let it process for 20 minutes. Adjust time for altitude differences. After the time is up, turn off the heat and remove the canner's lid. Let it stand for five minutes before removal.
9. To remove the jars, use your jar lifter and let them cool for 24 hours before checking the seal.
10. Enjoy your strawberry syrup!

Best Blueberry Syrup Around

Since blueberries are one of the healthiest fruits to eat, it is smart to incorporate them into your morning pancakes. This recipe is a healthy alternative to regular maple syrup that has a higher level of sugar. Blueberries are one of the only naturally occurring blue foods. The anthocyanin in the fruit causes its unique color. To reiterate the properties I mentioned in the Blasting Blueberries recipe of Chapter 4, anthocyanin lowers the risk of cancer and helps with insulin production. You can also check out the recipe mentioned above for more information on the harvesting of this amazing fruit.

Amount: One pint jar

Ingredients: *(See page 172 for Measurement Conversion)*

- 5 cups blueberries
- 1 cup sugar
- 2 teaspoons bottled lemon juice
- 2 ½ tablespoons Clear Jel
- ⅓ cup water

Directions:

1. Prepare all the canning equipment. Wash the jars and sterilize them if necessary. Add water to the canner but wait to boil.
2. In a large pot, add blueberries and 1/2 cup of water. Boil for 10 minutes and then let simmer for 20 minutes. Lightly stir to extract juice.
3. Put the berries in a jelly bag to let drip for 1 hour.

4. In a large pot, measure out 2 cups of blueberry juice and add sugar and lemon juice. Bring blueberry mixture to a boil, stirring to dissolve sugar.
5. In a separate small bowl combine water with the Clear Jel and stir until it's smooth. Add to boiling mixture. Stir for one minute.
6. Funnel the syrup into a heated jar, leaving ¼ inch of space. Wipe the jar's rim and put on the lid.
7. Using a jar lifter, gently place the jars in the canner, making sure there are 1-2 inches of water above them.
8. Bring the canner to a boil and let it process for 15 minutes. Adjust time for altitude differences. After the time is up, turn off the heat and remove the canner's lid. Let it stand for five minutes before removal.
9. To remove the jars, use your jar lifter and let them cool for 24 hours before checking the seal.
10. Enjoy your blueberry syrup!

More Sauces

Can't Be Beat Cranberry Sauce

When it comes to holiday dinners, cranberry sauce has a chokehold on the market. What is Thanksgiving or Christmas without this iconic sauce? Not only will it invoke festive cheer but it's also full of nutritional value. The holidays are the worst time for a diet so implementing a healthy side will limit any post dinner regrets. Since it's low in fat, cranberry sauce is good for your heart. Most of the cranberries in the U.S. come from Massachusetts or Wisconsin. There are two ways to harvest the fruit, dry and wet. Dry harvest is the fresh marketplace cranberries that are used in the recipe below. The wet method, which involves a bog, is used mainly for cranberry juice production.

Amount: Five pint jars

Ingredients: *(See page 172 for Measurement Conversion)*

- 3 lbs fresh cranberries
- 2 cups water
- 2 oranges, juiced and zested
- 1 lemon, juiced and zested
- 4 cups white granulated sugar
- 1 cinnamon sticks
- 2 tablespoons whole cloves
- Pinch of salt

Directions:

1. Prepare all the canning equipment. Wash the jars and sterilize them if necessary. Add water to the canner but wait to boil.
2. In a large pot, combine cranberries, sugar, water, orange zest and juice, lemon zest and juice, and a pinch of salt. Bring to a boil over high heat. Stir frequently.

3. Once a boil has been reached, add the cheese cloth filled with cinnamon and cloves. Continue to boil over high heat for 10-15 minutes. The cranberries should all pop.
4. Once all the cranberries have popped and your desired consistency has been reached remove the pot from the heat. Skim off any foam on the top.
5. Funnel the sauce into a heated jar, leaving ¼ inch of space. Wipe the jar's rim and put on the lid.
6. Using a jar lifter, gently place the jars in the canner, making sure there are 1-2 inches of water above them.
7. Bring the canner to a boil and let it process for 10 minutes. Adjust time for altitude differences.
8. After the time is up, turn off the heat and remove the canner's lid. Let it stand for five minutes before removal.
9. To remove the jars, use your jar lifter and let them cool for 24 hours before checking the seal.
10. Enjoy your cranberry sauce!

Hot Hot Sauce

The hot sauce that we use today has been around for nearly two centuries. Hot peppers are the key ingredient to making this spicy condiment. Hot peppers don't just provide heat to a dish, they also have some health benefits. The active chemical component of hot pepper is called "capsaicin." Capsaicin can help with sinus issues and can work as an antioxidant. Hot peppers grow best in warmer climates such as California but many gardeners have no problem growing their own. You can harvest your hot peppers 60 to 95 days after planting them. You'll know they are ready by their size and ripe color.

Amount: Four pint jars

Ingredients: *(See page 172 for Measurement Conversion)*

- 1 ½ cups hot peppers, chopped, stemmed and seeded
- 2 tablespoons pickling spice
- 8 cups tomatoes, diced
- 4 cups white vinegar
- 2 teaspoons pickling salt

Directions:

1. Prepare all the canning equipment. Wash the jars and sterilize them if necessary. Add water to the canner but wait to boil.
2. In a large pot, add in all ingredients. The spices should be in a spice bag or cheesecloth. Bring mixture to a boil, uncovered. Then let simmer, uncovered for 20 minutes.
3. Press mixture through a food mill.
4. Return the liquid to the pot. Bring to a full rolling boil, uncovered for 15 minutes.
5. Funnel the sauce into a heated jar, leaving ¼ inch of space. Wipe the jar's rim and put on the lid.

6. Using a jar lifter, gently place the jars in the canner, making sure there are 1-2 inches of water above them.
7. Bring the canner to a boil and let it process for 10 minutes. Adjust time for altitude differences.
8. After the time is up, turn off the heat and remove the canner's lid. Let it stand for five minutes before removal.
9. To remove the jars, use your jar lifter and let them cool for 24 hours before checking the seal.
10. Enjoy your hot sauce!

The Chicken Wing Sauce

There are so many different kinds of condiments to eat chicken wings with but none as bold as this one. The name alone declares itself as *the* chicken wing sauce. Its ingredients are very similar to barbecue sauce but the execution gives it a unique and perfect pairing for chicken. If you would prefer a healthier option, you can pair it with grilled chicken breast strips instead of the fried wings. You could also use vegan chicken or tofu as plant-based replacements if needed. If you're wondering more about the tomato, check out Chapter 6.

Amount: Four pint jars

Ingredients: *(See page 172 for Measurement Conversion)*

- 10 cups tomatoes, washed, peeled, cored, and chopped
- 2 cups onion, chopped

- ⅓ cup brown sugar
- ½ teaspoon cayenne pepper
- 1 ½ cups white vinegar
- 4 teaspoons salt
- 2 cloves garlic, minced
- 1 teaspoon allspice ground
- 1 teaspoon cinnamon ground
- 1 teaspoon cloves ground
- 1 teaspoon ginger ground

Directions:

1. Prepare all the canning equipment. Wash the jars and sterilize them if necessary. Add water to the canner but wait to boil.
2. In a large pot, add the tomatoes, onions, sugar, and cayenne. Bring to a boil uncovered. Let simmer uncovered for 30 minutes.
3. Remove from heat and let it cool before using a blender or food processor to puree the mixture.
4. Return mixture to the pot and add all the remaining ingredients. Bring to a boil then let simmer, uncovered, for an hour.
5. Funnel the sauce into a heated jar, leaving ½ inch of space. Wipe the jar's rim and put on the lid.
6. Using a jar lifter, gently place the jars in the canner, making sure there are 1-2 inches of water above them.
7. Bring the canner to a boil and let it process for 15 minutes. Adjust time for altitude differences.

8. After the time is up, turn off the heat and remove the canner's lid. Let it stand for five minutes before removal.
9. To remove the jars, use your jar lifter and let them cool for 24 hours before checking the seal.
10. Enjoy your chicken wing sauce!

Key Chapter 7 Takeaways

- Most condiments have been around for centuries.
- Ketchup was originally called catsup.
- Most dressings shouldn't be home canned.
- Syrup from fruit should be water bathed but maple syrup can seal on its own.
- Cranberry sauce is one of the healthiest options around the holidays.

Chapter 8: Bonus Chapter - Meals in a Jar

"To eat is a necessity, but to eat intelligently is an art."

- François de Rochefoucald

Meal Preparation

Meal preparation (prepping) is the practice of planning and preparing your meals ahead of time. Not only does it save time but many people utilize the practice for portion control. Nutrition can often take a back seat to the busy goings on of everyday life. This is an option for those who want to reach their health goals but just don't have the time. Nowadays it's easy to go out to your local fast-food joint instead of staying home and cooking a meal with nutritional value. In this fast world, we rarely have time to eat let alone the time to cook. Meal preparation can revolutionize your diet, keeping you healthy and happy.

In most meal prepping communities, Sunday is the day to plan and make your meals for the following week. This is fine if you want to waste your Sunday afternoon slaving away in a kitchen. With water bath canning, you can plan your food months ahead. This is called batch cooking where you only have to prepare food every couple of months. It's a great way to free up your days for more important activities. There are other methods to meal prepping such as individually portioned meals. This is where you portion the meal out and grab and go as you're hungry instead of eating the full prepared food. Another method is to prep the ingredient to cut down on cooking time but not fully eliminate it. Whichever method works best is ultimately up to you but I'm partial to my beloved water bath canner.

Before you start meal prepping make a list of what you want to achieve with it. This could be weight loss, dietary restrictions, getting nutrition value or anything else you want to do. This list will be the starting point to figure out what kind of meals you'll make to plan. If you're working towards portion control, you won't want to prepare too much food. You'll also want a variety of options for the week so you don't get stuck eating the same thing every day. It's also a good idea to pinpoint the times in your life you're most tempted to eat out or snack on unhealthy foods. Being prepared for these times can help you quit your unhealthy eating habits.

Meal preparation sounds great and all but where do you even start? Cooking the recipes from this book doesn't automatically help you eat healthier. Many of the recipes are condiments to meals, not actual entrees. How are you supposed to make a healthy and nutritious lunch out of pickled peaches? Don't worry I got you. In the next three sections I have prepared breakfast, lunch and dinner options. These are ways to turn water bath canned goods into an actual meal. It's important to know, this is just a jumping off point to help you start your healthy canning meal preparation. It's going to take your own research to come up with a variety of canning that works for your kitchen. Don't worry though, once you get a hold of what to do after the jar, meal prep will be life changing.

What's for Breakfast

Apple Butter on Toast

Apple butter on toast is an easy way to start your day. It only requires the two ingredients of apple butter and whole wheat toast. You can use white bread but whole wheat has less calories and more fiber. Simply spread the butter over your toast and voilà: breakfast is taken care of. So what is coming from your canning pantry? The apple butter. Grains can't be safely preserved so you should never can bread. Simply follow this recipe below to make sure you have a jar of apple in your reserves.

Amount: Three pint jars

Ingredients: *(See page 172 for Measurement Conversion)*

- 4 pounds of apples
- 1 cup of apple cider vinegar
- 2 cups water
- 4 cups of sugar
- 2 teaspoons cinnamon
- ½ teaspoon ground cloves
- ½ teaspoon allspice
- 1 tablespoon lemon zest
- 3 tablespoons lemon juice
- Pinch of salt

Directions:

1. Prepare all the canning equipment. Wash the jars and sterilize them if necessary. Add water to the canner but wait to boil.
2. When cutting up the apples don't peel or core them. Put them into a large pot and add apple cider vinegar and water. Cover and boil then simmer for 20 minutes to soften apples.
3. Put the mixture through a sieve or food mill.
4. Add the rest of the ingredients before putting in a pot and cooking it for 1 to 2 hours. It should be thick, smooth and dark brown in color.
5. Funnel the apple butter into a heated jar, leaving ¼ inch of space. Wipe the jar's rim and put on the lid.
6. Using a jar lifter, gently place the jars in the canner, making sure there are 1-2 inches of water above them.
7. Bring the canner to a boil and let it process for 10 minutes. Adjust time for altitude differences.
8. After the time is up, turn off the heat and remove the canner's lid. Let it stand for five minutes before removal.
9. To remove the jars, use your jar lifter and let them cool for 24 hours before checking the seal.
10. Enjoy your apple butter!

Greek Yogurt with Mango

Another healthy option for breakfast is Greek yogurt with Mango. If you're wondering why use Greek yogurt instead of regular yogurt, it's all about protein. Greek yogurt has half the carbs and sugar but twice the protein. After you've added your mango to the yogurt, feel free to top it off with granola for extra nutrients. So what's from the pantry? The mangos of course. As you know by now yogurt can't be processed and should come directly from the refrigerator. Follow the recipe below to can your mango topping.

Amount: Three pint jars

Ingredients: *(See page 172 for Measurement Conversion)*

- 8 or 9 mangoes, peeled and seeded
- 1/4 cup of sugar
- 2 cups of water
- 2 teaspoons lemon juice

Directions:

1. Prepare all the canning equipment. Wash the jars and sterilize them if necessary. Add water to the canner but wait to boil.
2. When cutting the mangos, you can leave them in larger halves or chop them up.

3. Pack the mangos into a heated jar, leaving ½ inch of space. Add in the lemon juice
4. In a pan, bring sugar and water to a boil. Stirring to dissolve.
5. Pour the syrup into the jars with the mangos in them. Wipe the jar's rim and put on the lid.
6. Using a jar lifter, gently place the jars in the canner, making sure there are 1-2 inches of water above them.
7. Bring the canner to a boil and let it process for 15 minutes. Adjust time for altitude differences.
8. After the time is up, turn off the heat and remove the canner's lid. Let it stand for five minutes before removal.
9. To remove the jars, use your jar lifter and let them cool for 24 hours before checking the seal.
10. Enjoy your mango!

What's for Lunch

Peach Salsa Tacos

Now that it's lunchtime, you're going to want something a little more filling. So why are we doing peach salsa and not regular salsa? Just because we can. If peach isn't the move for you, Chapter 6 has several other salsa options. To make these tacos just grill up your preferred meat (I like chicken), put it in a spinach or tortilla wrap and add your salsa. So what's from the pantry? The peach salsa of course. We all know a wrap from a can would be ridiculous but what about the meat? All fresh meat can be canned but only in a pressure canner. Water bath canning would be too dangerous due to meat's pH levels. Keep reading to find out how to make your own peach salsa.

Amount: Four pint jars

Ingredients: *(See page 172 for Measurement Conversion)*

- 6 cups of peaches, peeled and diced
- 1 cup of granulated sugar
- 1 cup of chopped red bell pepper
- 1 cup of apple cider vinegar
- ½ cup of chopped red onion
- ½ cup of cold water
- ¼ cup of lime juice
- ½ teaspoon kosher salt
- 2 jalapeño peppers, seeded and finely chopped
- 2 garlic cloves, minced
- 1 habanero pepper, seeded and minced
- ¼ cup chopped fresh cilantro

Directions:

1. Prepare all the canning equipment. Wash the jars and sterilize them if necessary. Add water to the canner but wait to boil.
2. In a Dutch oven, add in all the ingredients except cilantro.
3. Bring to a boil and stir until sugar has dissolved. Let it simmer, uncovered, for five minutes.

4. Remove the mixture from the heat source and stir in the cilantro.
5. Funnel the salsa into a heated jar, leaving ½ inch of space.
6. Wipe the jar's rim and put on the lid. Using a jar lifter, gently place the jars in the canner, making sure there are 1-2 inches of water above them.
7. Bring the canner to a boil and let it process for 15 minutes. Adjust time for altitude differences.
8. After the time is up, turn off the heat and remove the canner's lid. Let it stand for five minutes before removal.
9. To remove the jars, use your jar lifter and let them cool for 24 hours before checking the seal.
10. Enjoy your peach salsa!

Cowboy Candy Over Salmon

Candy for lunch? Sorry to disappoint but no. These are healthy options, remember? "Cowboy Candy" is just a nickname for candied jalapenos. They have no more sugar in them than most of the other recipes in this book. This meal is just as it sounds, candied jalapenos over grilled Alaskan salmon. If you want to use another type of fish, feel free. Salmon is just my preference since it's one of, if not the, healthiest fish to eat. As long as you're getting protein, it doesn't really matter what meat or meat substitute you use. So what's from the pantry? As you can tell from the recipe below, Cowboy Candy is water bath canner approved.

Amount: Three pints

Ingredients: *(See page 172 for Measurement Conversion)*

- 1 pound fresh jalapeños/21 peppers
- 2 cups white sugar
- ⅔ cup apple cider vinegar
- 1 teaspoon garlic powder
- ½ teaspoon celery seed
- ½ teaspoon ground turmeric
- ¼ teaspoon red pepper flakes

Directions:

1. Prepare all the canning equipment. Wash the jars and sterilize them if necessary. Add water to the canner but wait to boil.
2. Wear gloves when cutting the jalapenos into small rounds.
3. In a medium pot, add the sugar, apple cider vinegar, garlic powder, celery seed, turmeric, and red pepper flakes. Bring to a rolling boil before letting it simmer for 5 minutes.
4. Stir in the jalapenos and bring the mixture back to a boil. Let simmer for 10 minutes.
5. Remove jalapenos from the syrup and put them into a heated jar. Pour in the syrup, leaving ¼ inch of space. Wipe the jar's rim and put on the lid.
6. Using a jar lifter, gently place the jars in the canner, making sure there are 1-2 inches of water above them.

7. Bring the canner to a boil and let it process for 15 minutes. Adjust time for altitude differences.
8. After the time is up, turn off the heat and remove the canner's lid. Let it stand for five minutes before removal.
9. To remove the jars, use your jar lifter and let them cool for 24 hours before checking the seal.
10. Enjoy your candied jalapenos!

What's for Dinner

Spaghetti with Zoodles

I hope you're hungry because we are having spaghetti zoodles for dinner tonight. You may be thinking, why zoodles? I've been eating healthy all day, can't I just for once have my carbs? Sure. I mean, I'm just the person who wrote this book, I can't stop you from enjoying your pasta. I can make you feel bad about it though. Zoodles are an amazing alternative to grained pasta. Not only are they low in calories but they are packed full of vitamins and antioxidants. Whether or not they can be canned is still up in the air. The USDA doesn't recommend it but there are still recipes available. So that means the spaghetti sauce is what we're canning today. The recipe below is a little different from the pasta la vista sauce in chapter 6 but either one will work.

Amount: Four quart jars

Ingredients: *(See page 172 for Measurement Conversion)*

- 12 cups of tomatoes, peeled, drained, and chopped
- 1 cup green bell pepper, finely chopped
- 1 cup red bell pepper, finely chopped
- 2 cups of onions, finely chopped
- 18 ounces of tomato paste
- ½ cup vegetable
- ½ cup granulated sugar
- 3 tablespoons salt
- 2 tablespoons garlic, finely minced
- 1 ½ tablespoons dried oregano
- 1 ½ tablespoons dried basil
- 1 ½ teaspoons dried parsley
- 2 teaspoons Worcestershire sauce
- ½ cup lemon juice

Directions:

1. Prepare all the canning equipment. Wash the jars and sterilize them if necessary. Add water to the canner but wait to boil.
2. In a large pot, combine all ingredients except lemon juice.
3. Stir and bring to a boil. Let simmer for one hour.
4. When that's finished let it cool before blending the mixture until smooth.

5. Add the lemon juice to the bottom of a heated jar then add the sauce, leaving ½ inch of space. Wipe the jar's rim and put on the lid.
6. Using a jar lifter, gently place the jars in the canner, making sure there are 1-2 inches of water above them.
7. Bring the canner to a boil and let it process for 40 minutes. Adjust time for altitude differences.
8. After the time is up, turn off the heat and remove the canner's lid. Let it stand for five minutes before removal.
9. To remove the jars, use your jar lifter and let them cool for 24 hours before checking the seal.
10. Enjoy your spaghetti sauce!

Pickled Beets Salad

For a lighter option, we have pickled beet salad on the menu tonight. This consists of pickled beets, home canned to perfection, poured over a leafy green base and sprinkled with walnuts and feta cheese. Besides the pickled beets, none of the other ingredients are canned and are far superior when they are as fresh as possible. Follow the recipe below so that you can create this fancy entree that's perfect for dinner parties.

Amount: Six pint jars

Ingredients: *(See page 172 for Measurement Conversion)*

- 35 -40 small beets, unpeeled

- 2 cups sugar
- 2 cups water
- 2 cups white vinegar
- 1 teaspoon ground cloves
- 1 teaspoon allspice
- 1 tablespoon cinnamon
- 1 teaspoon whole cloves

Directions:

1. Prepare all the canning equipment. Wash the jars and sterilize them if necessary. Add water to the canner but wait to boil.
2. In a large pot cook the beets until they are tender.
3. Let them cool before removing the skins and cutting them into cubes.
4. In a saucepan, combine the rest of the ingredients and bring them to a boil. Let simmer for 10 minutes.
5. Put the beets into a heated jar and pour in the syrup, leaving ¾ inch of space. Wipe the jar's rim and put on the lid.
6. Using a jar lifter, gently place the jars in the canner, making sure there are 1-2 inches of water above them.
7. Bring the canner to a boil and let it process for 12 minutes. Adjust time for altitude differences.
8. After the time is up, turn off the heat and remove the canner's lid. Let it stand for five minutes before removal.

9. To remove the jars, use your jar lifter and let them cool for 24 hours before checking the seal.
10. Enjoy your pickled beets!

Key Chapter 8 Takeaways

- Meal preparation is a great option for monitoring what you eat.
- There are several methods to this practice including canning foods in bulk so you only have to prepare and plan every couple of months.
- Can a variety of options to avoid canning fatigue.
- For a more diverse diet, it's important to pair canned goods with goods that can't be canned in a water bath when eating them.
- While many water bath canning recipes include sugar there are still healthy ways to prepare the food.

Chapter 9
Everything Else you Need to Know

"Knowledge has no value unless you put it into practice."

-Anton Chekhov

Altitude

Water Bath Canning Chart

Altitude	Increase in Processing time
sea level	no adjustment
1,001-3,000	5 min
3,001 -6,000	10 min
6,001 - 8,000	15 min
8,001 - 10,000	20 min

Chart of the 20 largest cities in the U.S. and their Altitudes

City	State	Altitude	Rank by population
Phoenix	Arizona	1086 ft	5
Denver	Colorado	948 ft	19
Columbus	Ohio	902 ft	15

Charlotte	North Carolina	761 ft	16
Indianapolis	Indiana	719 ft	17
Fort Worth	Texas	653 ft	13
San Antonio	Texas	650 ft	7
Chicago	Illinois	597 ft	3
Dallas	Texas	430 ft	9
Austin	Texas	425 ft	11
Washington	D.C.	409 ft	20
Los Angeles	California	305 ft	2
Seattle	Washington	174 ft	18
Houston	Texas	105 ft	4
San Jose	California	82 ft	10
San Diego	California	62 ft	8
San Francisco	California	52 ft	14
Philadelphia	Pennsylvania	39 ft	6
New York City	New York	33 ft	1
Jacksonville	Florida	16 ft	12

5 cities with the highest altitudes in the U.S.

City	State	Altitude
Alma	Colorado	10,361 ft
Leadville	Colorado	10,150 ft
Blue River	Colorado	10,020 ft
Breckenridge	Colorado	9,600 ft
Flagstaff	Arizona	6,910 ft

Altitude of the 10 largest cities in Canada

City	Province	Altitude	Rank by population
Vancouver,	British Columbia	6,562 ft	8
Calgary	Alberta	3,428 ft	3
Edmonton	Alberta	2,116 ft	5
Hamilton	Ontario	1083 ft	10
Winnipeg	Manitoba	784 ft	7
Montreal	Quebec	764 ft	2
Brampton	Ontario	715 ft	9
Mississauga	Ontario	512 ft	6
Toronto	Ontario	251 ft	1
Ottawa	Ontario	230 ft	4

Measurement Conversion

Cups	Tablespoons	Teaspoons	Milliliters
		1 tsp	5 ml
1/16 cups	1 tbsp	3 tsp	15 ml
⅛ cups	2 tbsp	6 tsp	30 ml
¼ cups	4 tbsp	12 tsp	60 ml
⅓ cups	5 ⅓ tbsp	16 tsp	80 ml
½ cups	8 tbsp	24 tsp	120 ml
⅔ cups	10 ⅔ tbsp	32 tsp	160ml
¾ cups	12 tbsp	36 tsp	180 ml
1 cup	16 tbsp	48 tsp	240 ml

1 Gallon = 4 quarts = 8 pints =16 cups= 120 oz = 3.8 liters

1 Quart = 2 pints= 4 cups = 32 oz = 950 ml

1 Pint = 2 cups= 16 oz = 480 ml

1 cup = 8oz= 240ml

Cooking Temperatures

Fahrenheit = (Celsius x 1.8) +32

Celsius = (Fahrenheit - 32) x 0.5556

Pounds to Kilograms

1 lb = 0.45 kg					1 kg = 2.22 lbs

2 lbs = 0.90 kg					2 kg = 4.44 lbs

3 lbs = 1.35 kg					3 kg = 6.67 lbs

4 lbs = 1.80 kg					4 kg = 8.89 lbs

5 lbs = 2.25 kg					5 kg = 11.11 lbs

6 lbs = 2.70 kg					6 kg = 13.33 lbs

7 lbs = 3.15 kg					7 kg = 15.56 lbs

8 lbs = 3.60 kg					8 kg = 17.78 lbs

9 lbs = 4.05 kg					9 kg = 20.00 lbs

10 lbs = 4.50 kg				10 kg = 22.22 lbs

EWG's 2021 "Dirty Dozen"

1. Strawberries
2. Spinach
3. Kale, collard and mustard greens
4. Nectarines
5. Apples
6. Grapes
7. Cherries
8. Peaches
9. Pears
10. Bell and hot peppers
11. Tomatoes
12. Celery

EWG's 2021 "Clean Fifteen"

1. Avocados
2. Sweet corn
3. Pineapples
4. Onions
5. Papayas
6. Sweet peas (frozen)
7. Eggplants
8. Asparagus
9. Broccoli
10. Cabbages
11. Kiwis
12. Cauliflower
13. Mushrooms
14. Honeydew melons
15. Cantaloupes

Fruit and Tomato Canning Charts

Water Bath Canning Fruit Chart

Fruit type	Pack style	Pints	Quarts
apples	hot	20 min	20 min
apricots	raw	25 min	30 min
berries	raw	15 min	20 min
cherry	raw	20 min	25 min
fruit juice	hot	15 min	15 min
fruit jam	hot	10 min	10 min

peaches	hot	20 min	25 min
pears	hot	20 min	25 min
plums	hot	20 min	25 min
rhubarb	hot	10 min	10 min

Water Bath Canning Tomato Chart

Tomato type	Pack style	Pints	Quarts
crushed	hot	45 min	55 min
whole	hot/raw	50 min	55 min
juice	hot	45 min	50 min
sauce	hot	45 min	50 min

Water Bath Canning Pickled Chart

Pickled type	Pack style	Pints	Quarts
dill pickle	raw	15 min	20 min
sweet pickle	raw	10 min	15 min
pickle relish	hot	10 min	Not recommended
bread and butter pickles	hot	15 min	15 min
pickled beets	hot	40 min	40 min

Pesticides

Around 70% of non-organically grown produce in the United States contains residue from pesticides. This residue can be potentially harmful to humans and doesn't go away even after washing and peeling. Of this 90%, 70% was shown to have traces of more than one type of pesticide. Don't let this scare you off from consuming your fruit and vegetables, though. Shopping organically is an easy way to assure your produce is pesticide-free. Consider attending any local farmer markets instead of hitting up big chain marts. The Environmental Working Group (EWG) has compiled a list of the produce that contains the most pesticides. This list is aptly named the dirty dozen. If you're curious as to the produce with the least amount of pesticides, they have also provided a "Clean Fifteen." Both lists from 2021 are provided below.

What Can Go Wrong?

Don't worry, as long as you're a competent cook, you'll probably never have to deal with a kitchen fire. It would be very difficult to set boiling water on fire. You're more likely to have an issue while preparing the food in a saucepan or pot than when using your water bath canner. If you do end up with a tiny fire in your pan, do not try to put it out with water. Grease fires can be taken down by turning off the heat and smoothing the flames with a lid. Don't attempt to move the pan or hot grease could splash you. If you tend to be accident prone, invest in a fire extinguisher.

Water bath canners are very safe as long as they are used correctly. The worst thing that could happen is the lid somehow comes off. Water bath canners process food through the temperature of boiling water. If the lid comes undone you could be splashed by this boiling water and receive severe burns. You could also get burned by any steam that comes out. If the lid falls off, back away from any splash zone and try to kill the heat source. This might seem like it goes without saying but don't ever stick your hand in the water when the heat source is on. The temperature of boiling water is 212 °F. That will be very painful. If you do end up with a minor burn, apply cold water to the area. Any serious burn , seek a medical professional.

The last thing you should look out for is botulism. This is a serious illness that could result in death. Symptoms of botulism include difficulty breathing, blurry vision, nausea, slurred speech, droopy eyelids and even paralysis. Symptoms will usually appear within 18 to 36 hours after exposure. It is very important to seek medical attention immediately if you have any of these symptoms. Even after receiving medical treatment, paralysis can last months following the infection. If not treated right away this can be permanent. Some patients have reported breathing problems and fatigue years afterwards as well. The toxin that causes botulism attacks the nervous system and kills 5 out of every 100 people. Luckily the condition is rare and as long as you know how to avoid it, you'll probably never have to worry about it.

So how do you avoid this? Only use the water bath canner for its intended product. Vegetables with low acid will not be successfully canned in a water bath canner. If you are curious about a certain product and can't find a definitive answer on if it can be safely canned, don't do it. It's better to be safe than sorry. If something doesn't seal properly, you can try to can it again but older goods with a faulty seal should be thrown away. You should also look out for discoloration, foul smells or rotten fat deposits. These are all signs of a weak seal and contamination. Don't play roulette with your health. Follow the USDA and FDA guidelines even if it may seem inconvenient at times. They are there to maintain us as safe canners.

Conclusion

"You don't have to be great to start but you have to start to be great."

- Zig Ziglar

Congratulations, you have made it to the end of the book. An impressive feat considering all the puns you have had to endure. I truly hope you have enjoyed these recipes as much as I have. I believe the quote above is just the right sentiment to end this book on. You don't have to be a dietitian or a good cook to start your canning journey. You can be a certified kitchen disaster and still learn how to make a fantastic mango chutney. It just takes practice and a whole lot of patience. Remember, this is your path to make not follow. Nobody starts off their canning journey as a professional. There's a reason why the USDA doesn't approve of old pickling recipes. Perfection takes time and perhaps more importantly research. You'll get there and when you do, you'll be eating like a champion.

Even if you're only canning for your family, you're still making a huge difference. When you start canning, you start taking accountability for your waste habits. The only thing that can't be reused is the metal lids of the jars since they can't seal right the second time. While we can hope that this tiny issue can be fixed in a few years as canning practices evolve, there are still options for today. The metal lids don't have to contribute to your waste as they are recyclable. You can also reuse them as lids for refrigerated homemade food. If you do this make sure you store the lids in a way that doesn't confuse which ones can be canned. You don't want to waste any by ruining a seal.

There are alternatives to the metal lids as well. You may want to invest in some BPA free plastic lids. BPA just refers to the industrial chemical bisphenol A that seeps into food from the plastic. It could cause potential harm to infants and children so it's important not to only get BPA free plastic. Though they aren't as widely used as the metal ones, plastic lids have unlimited uses. If you choose this option remember that it is contributing to the creation of unnecessary plastic so buy responsibly. You could also use glass as an alternative but it runs the risk of chipping and putting broken glass in your food. They are indefinitely reusable like the plastic ones though. Whichever method you go with, make sure you recycle any waste so your canning can help the world as much as it helps you.

There are going to be some unavoidable expenses when you first start canning. Water bath canning is a cheaper alternative to other methods but you'll still need a large pot, jars, lids, and other equipment. You'll also have to worry about the price of the ingredients you'll be using. This will be your first investment. Stocking up on home canned goods may seem expensive at the moment but it'll save you money in the long run. As long as you utilize canning to the best of your ability you'll make your money back through limiting your annual food spoilage. If you sell your home canned goods, like many canners do, you'll make it back even faster as long as you find your market.

The next investment is time. I've said it once, I've said it a million times but it is sincerely the most important thing. Research everything. Call up your local extension service, haunt the USDA or FDA's websites and can your heart out. If the point of canning is to save time, why should you be spending all this time on it? Like I said, it's an investment. Spend time now, save time in the future. While you still should keep tabs on any changes for the home canning guidelines, canning will become so easy that you won't even think twice about it once you get all your research out of the way.

Despite the limitation on what can be processed, there are still many amazing recipes you can make with your water bath canner. The best place to start would be with a simple fruit canning recipe. They only have a few directions and one or two ingredients. Once you've tested the waters move on to something harder like a jam or jelly. Condiments are going to take more ingredients to really explore their favors. Canning these will be a fun place to start your transition into harder to make goods such as pickles and relish. Just like with any activity, it's better to start slow and work your way up.

With the 60 compiled recipes in this book, you are well on your way to a diverse and delicious panty. Diverse is the key aspect to being successful with home canning. Having options will help you eat healthier. It may seem easy to just can one recipe in bulk but it could result in canning fatigue. You don't want to get sick of eating a specific food and end up wasting all your work. As most dietitians will tell you, you should be receiving a variety of vitamins each day. This should be reflected in your canning habits. A water bath canner is a great start but you can also invest in a pressure canner for more diversity. With a pressure canner, you can process meat and regular vegetables ending with a more rounded out pantry.

It looks as if we have reached the end of the book, dear reader. I hope you can take the information you have learned and make wonderful things. Remember to have fun and try new recipes whenever you can. If you fail, the next batch will be better. As cliche as it may sound it's very crucial that you don't give up. If people gave up preservation hundreds of years ago we might never have had pickles. We would be in a real pickle then. Sorry, one last pun for the road. I wish you the best of luck and the most delicious food.

Thank You

Dear reader, I would like to take this time to appreciate you. Without your purchase and interest, I wouldn't be able to keep writing helpful books like this one. Once again, THANK YOU for reading this book. I hope you enjoyed it as much as I enjoyed writing it.

Before you go, I have a small favor to ask of you. **Would you please consider posting a review of this book on the platform? Posting a review will help support my writing.**

Your feedback is very important and will help me continue to provide more informative literature in the future. I look forward to hearing from you. Just follow this relevant link below.

>> Click Here to leave a review on Amazon US <<

>> Click Here to leave a review on Amazon UK <<

>> Click Here to leave a review on Amazon Canada <<

>> Click Here to leave a review on Amazon Mexico <<

>> Click Here to leave a review on Amazon Brazil <<

>> Click Here to leave a review on Amazon Spain <<

>> Click Here to leave a review on Amazon Italy <<

>> Click Here to leave a review on Amazon France <<

>> Click Here to leave a review on Amazon India <<

Glossary

Acid — Any sour compounds.

Antioxidant — The citric acid of lemon or lime juice, ascorbic acid or a blend of citric and ascorbic acids, that stops oxidation and browning. It also has health properties.

Artificial sweeteners — Synthetic alternatives to sugar. Sweetness can vary.

Brine — salt water solution that is used to pickle fruits and vegetables.

Bacteria — Microorganisms that can be potentially harmful. In canning, bacteria thrives in low acid foods and if not properly processed.

Blanching — Preparation method that boils vegetables or fruit before emerging them in ice water to elongate the food's quality.

Botulism — A potentially fatal illness that attacks the nerves and can cause paralysis.

Canning — Preserving produce in jars by heating it up and killing any bacteria.

Canning rack — Rack used at the bottom of a cooker to elevate the jars from the pot.

Cheesecloth — A woven cloth that can be used to strain juice or infuse herbs and spices during the cooking process.

Chutney — slow cooked fruits or vegetables with the addition of spices such as garlic, ginger or chilies. This dish originates from India.

Clean Fifteen — EGW's list for the top fifteen types of produce that are unlikely to have pesticides.

Condiment — A sweet or savory sauce used to enhance flavors of other food.

Dirty dozen — EGW's list for the top twelve produces that are most likely to have pesticide residue

EPA — An acronym for Environmental protection agency. The mission of this independent executive agency of the United States is to protect the environment and human health.

EGW — An acronym for Environmental Working Group. This activist organization works in researching agricultural populations. Every year they provide a produce pesticide lists called the "dirty dozen" "clean fifteen"

FDA — An acronym for The Food and Drug Administration. This federal agency of the department of health and human services is in charge of food and drug regulations with the goal of protecting and maintaining public health and safety.

Food mill — three part food preparation utensil for sieving and mashing foods. The parts are a bowl, a bottom plate with holes, and a crank with a metal blade that crushes the food and forces it through the holes in the plate.

Hot packing — Packing partially cooked food into jars and then covering them in boiling water, juice or syrup.

Jam — Crushed or chopped fruit that is cooked with sugar or pectin to a thickened but spreadable consistency.

Jar — Glass container used for processing in a canner. Comes in several sizes such as quart, pint and half pint. They have a two piece closure consisting of a metal lid and a band.

Jar lifter — A canning utensil used to place and remove jars from the canner safely.

Jelly — Fruit juice that has been strained from fruit and cooked with sugar or pectin to create a firmer consistency than Jam.

Marmalade — Preserve made from the peel and juice of citrus fruits boiled with sugar and water.

Meal Preparation — This is the process of creating meal plans by scheduling out dishes and preparing them ahead of time.

Pectin — A carbohydrate found in fruits and vegetables that deteriorates as they ripen. This is why produce becomes soft and loses its structure. You can also buy pectin in powdered and liquid forms to make jams, jellies and other soft spreads.

Pesticides — Substance applied to plants that kills and repels insects and other potentially harmful ailments.

pH levels — A way to measure the acidic level of water on a range of 0-14. Seven is neutral, less than seven is acidic and more than seven is considered base.

Pickling — Preservation for produce through immersion in vinegar or anaerobic fermentation.

Pressure Canner — A special appliance that reaches higher temperatures than water bath canning. This is the only approved way to preserve low acid foods such as vegetables and meats.

Raw Packing — Packing uncooked food into jars and then covering them in boiling water, juice or syrup.

Rolling boil — A continuous and strong boil that churns the ingredients from high heat.

Simmer — gently bubbling liquid from a low heat source.

Sieve — A strainer made from a wired mesh used for making pulps, purees and juices.

Syrup — Refers to canning syrup made from sugar and water or juice. This liquid is added to canned produce to help them become processed.

USDA — An acronym for The United States Department of Agriculture. This federal department is responsible for creating and maintaining federal laws about agriculture and food in relation to safety and nutritional quality.

Water Bath Canner — A large pot with a rack that reaches high temperatures for boiling jars and preserving food. This process is only used for food products with high acidic levels.

Index

A

acidic, 18, 21, 84, 184
air bubbles, 68, 72
alkaline, 21
allspice, 54, 56, 131, 151, 156, 166
Apple Butter, 8, 156, 190
apple cider vinegar, 54, 56, 97, 112, 133, 156, 157, 160, 162
Apple-Solutely Delicious Jam, 41, 42, 78
Apricots, 93, 190
Asparagus, 174
Awesomesauce Applesauce, 78, 79

B

Baby Sauce, 116
balsamic vinegar, 93, 119
Barbecue Sauce, 132, 189
basil, 117, 119, 121, 164
bay leaves, 117, 119
Be Grape-Ful Jelly, 57
beets, unpeeled, 165
berries, 40, 77, 142, 145, 174
berry, 14, 40, 106, 195
black peppercorns, 86, 135
Blasting Blueberries, 66, 67, 76, 145
Bloody Mary, 126, 128, 191
blueberries, 27, 66, 67, 76, 77, 122, 144, 145, 190
Blueberry Syrup, 8, 144
boiling water, 60, 72, 176, 183, 184
bourbon, 133
Broccoli, 174

C

Cabbages, 174
canola oil, 116
Cantaloupes, 174
Cauliflower, 174
cauliflower florets, 89
cayenne pepper, 133, 151
celery seed, 99, 100, 162
celery,, 124, 127, 137
cherries, 65, 74, 75, 95
Cherry Bomb Pie Filling, 74, 76
cherry tomatoes, 107
Chicken Wing Sauce, 150
chili powder, 112
Chili Sauce, 136, 193
chopped onion, 52, 99
chutney, 24, 52, 53, 55, 56, 57, 62, 178, 190, 192
cider vinegar, 84, 99, 101, 140
cilantro, 110, 111, 112, 114, 160, 161
cinnamon, 71, 72, 75, 79, 80, 92, 94, 131, 137, 147, 148, 151, 156, 166, 193
Cinnamon Pear Sauce, 79, 81, 193
clove, 52, 56, 86
Cocktail, 95
coconut, 44
Condiments, 130, 136, 179
cored, 56, 71, 80, 110, 114, 150
coriander, 54
Cowboy Candy Over Salmon, 161
cranberries, 147, 148, 191
Cranberry Sauce, 146, 191
crystallized ginger, 52
cucumber, 97
cumin, 112, 114, 115
cups of sugar, 48, 69, 71, 156

D

dandelion petals, 59
Dandy Dandelion Jelly, 59
Diced Tomatoes, 104, 191

dill seeds, 86
dried rosemary, 119

E

ears of corn, 89
eggs, 140

F

fennel seeds, 119
flakes, 52, 116, 121, 133, 162
fruit juice, 40, 41, 61, 174

G

garlic, 52, 56, 86, 90, 110, 111, 112, 113, 114, 115, 116, 118, 121, 127, 132, 133, 135, 151, 160, 162, 164, 182
ginger, 54, 56, 137, 151, 182
Glad Marmalade, 46
golden raisins, 52, 54
Granny's Apple Pie Filling, 70
granulated sugar, 40, 46, 77, 143, 147, 160, 164
grapes, 57, 58
Greek Yogurt with Mango, 158
green bell pepper, 164
Grigio, 134, 135
ground black pepper, 54, 56, 112, 119
ground cloves, 156
ground coriander, 56

H

habanero pepper, 160
Harmony, 138
honey, 40, 41, 52, 53, 93, 94, 121, 140, 141, 189
Honeycrisp apples, 42
Honeydew melons, 174
Horseradish, 138, 190, 191
hot chili pepper, 54

Hot Sauce, 148, 191
husked, 114

J

jalapeño peppers, 160
jalapenos, 100, 101, 114, 161, 162, 163, 192
jalapeños, 162
jam, 24, 40, 41, 42, 43, 45, 62, 65, 141, 143, 174, 179, 189, 192, 193, 195
Jam Recipes, 40
jams, 20, 41, 184
Jams, 1, 4, 40
Jel, 71, 72, 73, 74, 75, 145, 146, 190
Jellies, 40
jelly, 24, 40, 57, 58, 59, 60, 61, 62, 65, 144, 145, 179, 192, 193
Jelly Recipes, 5, 57

K

kiwi, 69, 70
Krazy Kiwi, 69, 70

L

large pears, 80
lemon juice, 21, 42, 44, 46, 48, 60, 71, 72, 73, 75, 77, 80, 105, 107, 108, 117, 119, 121, 124, 125, 127, 143, 144, 145, 146, 156, 158, 159, 164, 165
Lemon Zest Blueberry Sauce, 76, 77
light brown sugar, 54, 56
lime juice, 160
low-acid foods, 21

M

Mango Chutney, 4, 52, 190
mangoes, 52, 158
Marinara Sauce, 118, 192
marmalade, 24, 46, 47, 48, 49, 50, 62, 76, 189, 191, 193, 195

Marmalade Recipes, 45
Marmalades, 40
Marry Me Mustard, 134
Meat, 20, 21, 116
Mild Salsa, 110
minced, 52, 114, 116, 118, 121, 127, 151, 160, 164
Mushrooms, 174
mustard seed, 99, 100, 134, 135, 137, 139
mustard seeds, whole, 52

O

olive oil, 118, 121
oranges, 46, 147, 193
oregano, 119, 121, 164

P

paprika, 114, 115, 133
parsley, 116, 124, 127, 164
Pasta La Vista, 116
pasta sauce, 116, 118, 120, 128
Peach Salsa Tacos, 159
peaches, 53, 54, 65, 91, 92, 93, 95, 155, 160, 175, 190, 193
Peachy Keen Chutney, 53, 92
Pear-Fect Chutney, 55, 79
pectin, 44, 46, 47, 58, 60, 61, 62, 77, 183, 184
Pectin, 40, 41, 184
peel, 46, 47, 54, 123, 143, 144, 157, 183
peeled, 49, 52, 54, 56, 71, 92, 110, 124, 132, 137, 150, 158, 160, 164
Persian limes, 49
Pesticides, 176, 184
Pickled Beets Salad, 165
Pickled Onions, 87
Pickled Peaches, 91, 190
pickles, 20, 83, 84, 85, 87, 97, 175, 180, 193, 195
Pickling, 83, 85, 102, 184
pickling cucumbers, 86
pickling spice, 149

Piña Coladas Jam, 43
Pinot, 134, 135
Pizza Sauce, 120, 191
Puns Jelly, 61
pureed pineapple, 44

R

raspberries, 67, 68, 192
red chili pepper, 52
red pepper flake, 117
Relish, 97, 99, 100, 189, 191, 192
rhubarb, 72, 73, 175, 190, 195
Rhubarb Pie Filling, 72, 190
ripe plums, 61
Rockin Raspberries, 67, 69
Roma tomatoes, 108, 128
rosemary, 135

S

sage, 119
salsa, 110, 111, 113, 115, 159, 161, 189, 191, 193, 195
Salsa Verde, 113, 189
salt, 54, 56, 84, 86, 87, 88, 90, 95, 96, 97, 98, 99, 100, 101, 107, 110, 111, 112, 114, 115, 116, 119, 121, 122, 123, 125, 127, 131, 133, 134, 135, 137, 138, 139, 147, 149, 151, 156, 160, 164, 182
Spaghetti, 163, 191, 192
Spicy Salsa, 111
strawberries, 13, 27, 38, 40, 41, 95, 141, 142, 143, 144, 195
Straw-Berry Good Jam, 40
Strawberry Vinaigrette, 141, 193
Sub-Lime Marmalade, 49

T

Thai chili, 114
thyme, 88, 119, 121
tomatillos, 113, 114, 115, 191

Tomato Juice, 122, 189
tomato puree, 121, 130
tomatoes, 189, 191, 192, 193
turmeric, 97, 98, 162

U

unsalted butter, 61

V

vegetables, 20, 21, 83, 85, 89, 90, 100, 102, 116, 124, 131, 133, 137, 176, 180, 182, 184, 190
vermouth, 93, 94
vinegar, 21

W

white onions, 112
white rum, 44
white sugar, 57, 80, 142, 162
white vinegar, 52, 86, 87, 88, 90, 92, 97, 110, 114, 137, 138, 142, 149, 151, 166
Whole Lotta Whole Tomato, 108
wine, 57, 134
Worcestershire sauce, 117, 127, 164

Y

yellow mustard seeds, 135
yogurt, 64, 76, 158

Z

zest, 49, 50, 77, 80, 147, 156
Zest Lemon Marmalade, 47
zested, 147
Zoodles, 163

References

10 Fun Facts About Tomatoes | Campbell's Soup UK. (2021, March 31). Campbell's Soup UK. https://www.campbellsoup.co.uk/blog/fun-facts-about-tomatoes/

Adamant, A. (2018a, July 7). *How to Can Mango*. Practical Self Reliance. https://practicalselfreliance.com/canning-mango/

Adamant, A. (2018b, October 15). *Canning Apple Pie Filling*. Practical Self Reliance. https://practicalselfreliance.com/canning-apple-pie-filling/

Adamant, A. (2019a, March 30). *Canning Maple Syrup for Long Term Preservation*. Practical Self Reliance. https://practicalselfreliance.com/canning-maple-syrup/#:~:text=Since%20syrup%20is%20so%20high

Adamant, A. (2019b, July 10). *Canning Cherry Pie Filling*. Practical Self Reliance. https://practicalselfreliance.com/canning-cherry-pie-filling/

Adamant, A. (2019c, September 21). *Apple Jam*. Practical Self Reliance. https://practicalselfreliance.com/apple-jam/

Adcock, D. (n.d.-a). *Honey Mustard-canning recipe Recipe - Food.com*. Www.food.com. Retrieved February 13, 2022, from https://www.food.com/recipe/honey-mustard-canning-recipe-69100

Adcock, D. (n.d.-b). *Jalapeno Pickle Relish Recipe - Food.com*. Www.food.com. Retrieved February 13, 2022, from https://www.food.com/recipe/jalapeno-pickle-relish-9407

Amanda. (2011, September 10). *Canning Salsa Verde, Made With Tomatillos • Heartbeet Kitchen*. Heartbeet Kitchen. https://heartbeetkitchen.com/tomatillosalsaverde/

Amanda. (2013, September 12). *Fiery Roasted Salsa: a canning recipe!* Heartbeet Kitchen. https://heartbeetkitchen.com/fiery-roasted-salsa/

Axe. (n.d.). *Tomato Juice - Canning Recipe - Food.com*. Www.food.com. https://www.food.com/recipe/tomato-juice-canning-188981

B, J. (2018, February 16). *Orange Marmalade / The Grateful Girl Cooks!* The Grateful Girl Cooks! https://www.thegratefulgirlcooks.com/orange-marmalade/#:~:text=The%20fruit%20is%20cooked%2C%20sugar

Ball. (2011). *Low Sugar / No Sugar Strawberry Jam*. Allrecipes. https://www.allrecipes.com/recipe/217924/low-sugar-no-sugar-strawberry-jam/

Ball, N. (n.d.). *Smoky-Sweet Barbecue Sauce Recipe by Tasty*. Tasty.co. Retrieved February 13, 2022, from https://tasty.co/recipe/smoky-sweet-barbecue-sauce

Balsamic Pickled Apricots. (n.d.). Better Homes & Gardens. Retrieved February 13, 2022, from https://www.bhg.com/recipe/balsamic-pickled-apricots-/

Barnes, D. (2021, March 17). *These 12 fruits and vegetables contain more pesticide residue than others, "Dirty Dozen" study says*. USA TODAY. https://www.usatoday.com/story/news/nation/2021/03/17/pesticides-these-fruits-and-vegetables-put-them-dirty-dozen-list/4707708001/

Bauer, B. A. (2016). *Tips to reduce your exposure to BPA*. Mayo Clinic. https://www.mayoclinic.org/healthy-lifestyle/nutrition-and-healthy-eating/expert-answers/bpa/faq-20058331

Bauer, E. (2021a, May 28). *Mango Chutney*. Simply Recipes. https://www.simplyrecipes.com/recipes/homemade_mango_chutney/

Bauer, E. (2021b, November 18). *Apple Butter*. Simply Recipes. https://www.simplyrecipes.com/recipes/apple_butter/

Belk, M. (2013, May 9). *Canning Kiwifruit*. ThriftyFun. https://www.thriftyfun.com/tf/Food_Tips_and_Info/Canning/Canning-Kiwifruit.html

Better Homes and Gardens. (n.d.). *Canned Applesauce*. Better Homes & Gardens. Retrieved February 12, 2022, from https://www.bhg.com/recipe/canned-applesauce/

Blue book services. (n.d.). *Pineapple – Produce Blue Book*. Blue Book Services. Retrieved February 12, 2022, from https://www.producebluebook.com/know-your-commodity/pineapple/#:~:text=Most%20U.S.%2Dgrown%20pineapple%20still

BLUEROWZE. (n.d.). *Nana's Southern Pickled Peaches*. Allrecipes. Retrieved February 13, 2022, from https://www.allrecipes.com/recipe/72126/nanas-southern-pickled-peaches/

Cameron, C. W. (2011, January 18). In Season: Lemons. *The Atlanta Journal-Constitution*. https://www.ajc.com/entertainment/dining/season-lemons/DZmIptJTgAJgrHLYAZo6aL/#:~:text=American%2Dgrown%20lemons%20are%20available

Canning blueberries. (2015, August 19). Healthy Canning. https://www.healthycanning.com/canning-blueberries

Canning Mixed Fruit - Better in a Jar! - SBCanning.com - homemade canning recipes. (n.d.). SBCanning. Retrieved February 13, 2022, from https://www.sbcanning.com/2013/03/canning-mixed-fruit-better-in-jar.html

Canning Pickled Horseradish - SBCanning.com - homemade canning recipes. (n.d.). SBCanning. Retrieved February 13, 2022, from https://www.sbcanning.com/2013/10/canning-pickled-horseradish.html

Canned Rhubarb Pie Filling. (2016, July 6). Healthy Canning. https://www.healthycanning.com/canned-rhubarb-pie-filling

Canning Syrups - Corn Syrup or Clear Jel which is the better texture? - SBCanning.com - homemade canning recipes. (2022). SBCanning. https://www.sbcanning.com/2013/11/canning-syrups-corn-syrup-or-clear-jel.html

Canning Terms Glossary. (2022). Google.com. https://www.google.com/url?q=https://www.freshpreserving.com/canning-terms-glossary.html&sa=D&source=docs&ust=1644771901875450&usg=AOvVaw2ZB

Centers for Disease Control and Prevention. (2019). *Symptoms*. Cdc.gov. https://www.cdc.gov/botulism/symptoms.html

Chicken wing sauce. (2016, September 14). Healthy Canning. https://www.healthycanning.com/chicken-wing-sauce

Chihak, S., April 27, R. U., & 2020. (2020, April 27). *Save Your Produce Up to a YearWhen You Master Water Bath Canning*. Better Homes & Gardens. https://www.bhg.com/recipes/how-to/preserving-canning/canning-basics/

Cook, S. (2021, August 7). *Dill Pickle Relish - {Canning Relish}*. Sustainable Cooks. https://www.sustainablecooks.com/dill-relish-canning-recipe-step-by-step/

Delany, A. (2018, March 20). *What Are Tomatillos, Anyway?* Bon Appétit. https://www.bonappetit.com/story/what-are-tomatillos

Easy Hot Sauce. (2016, August 24). Healthy Canning. https://www.healthycanning.com/easy-hot-sauce

Editors, L. C. (2021, August 7). *Peach Salsa*. Leite's Culinaria. https://leitesculinaria.com/105397/recipes-peach-salsa.html#recipe

Educational Resources. (n.d.). *Elevations of the 50 Largest Cities (by population, 1980 Census) | U.S. Geological Survey*. Www.usgs.gov. Retrieved February 12, 2022, from https://www.usgs.gov/educational-resources/elevations-50-largest-cities-population-1980-census

Elizabeth. (2021, August 3). *Cranberry Sauce for Canning*. The Jam Jar Kitchen. https://jamjarkitchen.com/2021/08/03/cranberry-sauce-for-canning/

Evans, R. (2014, December 24). *Lemon Marmalade - Canning for Christmas*. AT HOME with REBECKA. https://athomewithrebecka.com/lemon-marmalade-canning-for-christmas/

Food labels - Better Health Channel. (2020, February 25). Www.betterhealth.vic.gov.au. https://www.betterhealth.vic.gov.au/health/healthyliving/food-labels#list-of-ingredients-on-food-labels

Froment, L. (n.d.). *How Do Cranberries Grow*. Www.westfieldinsurance.com. Retrieved February 13, 2022, from https://www.westfieldinsurance.com/resources/articles/how-do-cranberries-grow#:~:text=Cranberries%20grow%20on%20the%20vines

Garden Vegetable Juice. (2017, September 1). Healthy Canning. https://www.healthycanning.com/garden-vegetable-juice

Garlicky Pickled Mixed Veggies. (n.d.). Better Homes & Gardens. Retrieved February 13, 2022, from https://www.bhg.com/recipe/garlicky-pickled-mixed-veggies/

Homemade Bloody Mary Mix - SBCanning.com - homemade canning recipes. (n.d.). SBCanning. Retrieved February 13, 2022, from https://www.sbcanning.com/2012/07/homemade-bloody-mary-mix.html

Homemade Canned Spaghetti Sauce. (n.d.). Taste of Home. Retrieved February 13, 2022, from https://www.tasteofhome.com/recipes/homemade-canned-spaghetti-sauce/

Horseradish. (n.d.). FoodPrint. Retrieved February 13, 2022, from https://foodprint.org/real-food/horseradish/

Huffstetler, E. (2018, November 21). *Can I Reuse My Canning Lids?* The Spruce Eats. https://www.thespruceeats.com/can-you-reuse-canning-lids-1389094

Jami. (2014, January 23). *Home Canned Pizza Sauce {from frozen or fresh tomatoes}*. An Oregon Cottage. https://anoregoncottage.com/home-canned-pizza-sauce/

Johnston, C. (2020, July 30). *How to Can Diced Tomatoes*. Wholefully. https://wholefully.com/can-diced-tomatoes/

KDP. (n.d.). *Pina Colada Jam Recipe - Food.com*. Www.food.com. Retrieved February 12, 2022, from https://www.food.com/recipe/pina-colada-jam-135040?mode=US&scaleto=5

Kelley. (2014, September 1). *Canning Week 2014 + How to Can Whole Raspberries*. Mountain Mama Cooks. https://mountainmamacooks.com/canning-week-2014-can-whole-raspberries/

Kelsey. (2021, October 16). How Many Cups In A Quart, Pint, Gallon (Free Printable). *Bake Me Some Sugar*. https://bakemesomesugar.com/how-many-cups-in-a-quart-pint-gallon/

Kim, A. (2016, May 26). *How To Make Dandelion Jelly*. Homestead Acres. https://www.homestead-acres.com/how-to-make-dandelion-jelly/

Kimberly. (2017, September 8). *BEST Marinara Sauce*. The Daring Gourmet. https://www.daringgourmet.com/best-marinara-sauce-for-canning/

KITTENCAL. (n.d.). *Pickled Beets (For Canning) Recipe - Food.com*. Www.food.com. Retrieved February 12, 2022, from https://www.food.com/recipe/pickled-beets-for-canning-177650

Lampkin, B. (2018, November 14). *10 Pickle Facts to Savor (in Honor of National Pickle Day)*. Mentalfloss.com. https://www.mentalfloss.com/article/71166/10-pickle-facts-savor-honor-national-pickle-day

Lee, M., Hutcheon, J., Dukan, E., & Milne, I. (2017). Rhubarb (Rheum species): the role of Edinburgh in its cultivation and development. *Journal of the Royal College of Physicians of Edinburgh, 47*(1), 102–109. https://doi.org/10.4997/jrcpe.2017.121

Lisa. (2018, September 8). *Homemade Plum Jelly*. The Cooking Bride. https://cookingbride.com/sauces-and-seasonings/homemade-plum-jelly/

Maria. (2017, September 23). *Canning Raw Pack Whole Tomatoes -a step by step guide*. She Loves Biscotti. https://www.shelovesbiscotti.com/canning-raw-pack-whole-tomatoes/

Mel. (2018, September 6). *Homemade Canned Spaghetti Sauce {Step-by-Step Tutorial}*. Mel's Kitchen Cafe. https://www.melskitchencafe.com/homemade-spaghetti-marinara-sauce-for-canning-or-freezing/

Melissa, A. (2015, May 26). *Secret Ingredients Not Listed on the Food Label*. ThirtySomethingSuperMom. https://thirtysomethingsupermom.com/secret-ingredients-not-listed-on-the-food-label/

Meredith, L. (2021a, May 4). *Homemade Spicy Peach Chutney*. The Spruce Eats. https://www.thespruceeats.com/peach-chutney-recipe-1327510

Meredith, L. (2021b, July 13). *How to Make and Can Sweet and Tangy Pear Chutney*. The Spruce Eats. https://www.thespruceeats.com/pear-chutney-recipe-1327511

Milisa. (2019, July 22). *Sweet Pickle Relish {Easy Canning Recipe}*. Miss in the Kitchen. https://www.missinthekitchen.com/sweet-pickle-relish/

Mobley, A. (2017, November 29). *Homemade Dijon Mustard Recipe*. Flour on My Face. https://flouronmyface.com/homemade-dijon-mustard-recipe/

Mock, S. (2020, August 5). *Candied Jalapeños Recipe (Cowboy Candy)*. Savoring the Good®. https://www.savoringthegood.com/candied-jalapenos/

Moreau, N. (2021, September 28). *Largest Cities in Canada by Population | The Canadian Encyclopedia*. Www.thecanadianencyclopedia.ca. https://www.thecanadianencyclopedia.ca/en/article/largest-cities-in-canada-by-population

Myrick, R. (2011, August 11). *Ketchup Fun Facts | Mobile Cuisine*. Mobile Cuisine | Food Truck, Pop up & Street Food Coverage. https://mobile-cuisine.com/did-you-know/ketchup-fun-facts/#:~:text=Heinz%20Company%20back%20in%201876

Nguyen, S. (2021, May 2). *Everything you need to know about when pears are in season*. HappySprout. https://www.happysprout.com/inspiration/pears-in-season-when/#:~:text=Pears%20are%20typically%20available%20from

oldworldgardenfarms. (2021, July 27). *How To Make The Best Canned Salsa - Our Tried & True Recipe*. Old World Garden Farms. https://oldworldgardenfarms.com/2021/07/27/best-canned-salsa-recipe/

Patterson, H. (2017, June 6). *What's in Season: Limes - Farm Flavor*. Farmflavor.com. https://farmflavor.com/lifestyle/home/whats-season-limes/#:~:text=Limes%20are%20usually%20at%20their

Peaches. (2021, September). Www.agmrc.org. https://www.agmrc.org/commodities-products/fruits/peaches#:~:text=As%20of%202017%2C%20peaches%20are

Peterson, S. (2021, February 19). *Water Bath Canning with Printable Checklist. How to Use Your Canner*. SimplyCanning. https://www.simplycanning.com/water-bath-canning/#whatisit

Peterson, S. (2020, April 25). *How to Can Homemade Ketchup: A Safe Recipe for a Water Bath Canner*. SimplyCanning. https://www.simplycanning.com/homemade-ketchup/

Petre, A. (2020, December 14). *How to Meal Prep — A Beginner's Guide*. Healthline. https://www.healthline.com/nutrition/how-to-meal-prep#choosing-meals

Pickled Sweet Onions. (n.d.). Taste of Home. Retrieved February 13, 2022, from https://www.tasteofhome.com/recipes/pickled-sweet-onions/

Preserve, B. H. S., Learn to. (2014, October 21). *Cinnamon Pear Sauce*. USA Pears. https://usapears.org/recipe/cinnamon-pear-sauce/

Blueberry Lemon Dessert Sauce {Water Bath Canning Recipe}. Its Yummi. https://www.itsyummi.com/blueberry-lemon-dessert-sauce/#recipe

Sertich Velie, M. (2018, August 10). *What's the Difference Between Jam, Jelly, Compote, and Conserve?* Serious Eats. https://www.seriouseats.com/difference-between-jam-jelly-compote-conserve-apple-butter-preserves-types

Shawn. (2021, June 1). *Homemade Dill Pickles Recipe*. I Wash You Dry. https://iwashyoudry.com/homemade-canned-dill-pickles/

Strawberry Vinaigrette. (2017, December 21). Healthy Canning. https://www.healthycanning.com/strawberry-vinaigrette

Sweet Chili Sauce - SBCanning.com - homemade canning recipes. (2022). SBCanning. https://www.sbcanning.com/2012/07/sweet-chili-sauce.html

Sweetser, R. (2021, June 29). *Canning for Beginners: What Is Canning?* Old Farmer's Almanac. https://www.almanac.com/canning-for-beginners

The Hale Groves Team. (2019, September 23). *Why are Florida Oranges different from California Oranges? | Farm Fresh Fruit Gifts*. Hale Groves. https://www.halegroves.com/blog/why-are-florida-oranges-different-from-california-oranges/#:~:text=Florida%20and%20California%20are%20well

Traister, L. (2021, September 12). *Canning Cherry Tomatoes (Two Simple Ways)*. Lady Lee's Home. https://ladyleeshome.com/canning-cherry-tomatoes/

Treiber, L. (2017, August 7). *Processing methods for pickled products*. MSU Extension. https://www.canr.msu.edu/news/processing_methods_for_pickled_products

Trowbridge Filippone, P. (2021, December 26). *How to Make Lime Marmalade With 3 Ingredients*. The Spruce Eats. https://www.thespruceeats.com/lime-marmalade-recipe-1808111

University, U. S. (n.d.). *Food Safety & Nutrition*. Extension.usu.edu. Retrieved February 12, 2022, from https://extension.usu.edu/saltlake/home-family-food/food-safety-preservation

USDA. (n.d.). *Food Waste FAQs*. Www.usda.gov. https://www.usda.gov/foodwaste/faqs#:~:text=In%20the%20United%20States%2C%20food

Wisconsin department of public instruction. (n.d.). *Mango History*. USDA. https://dpi.wi.gov/sites/default/files/imce/school-nutrition/pdf/fact-sheet-mango.pdf

Images

Biro-Horvath, R. (2019). [Untitled online image of pickles in a jar]. Unsplash. https://unsplash.com/photos/4MKPaMGIA3U

Chung, Z. (2020). Gardener harvesting apples with daughter in garden [Online image]. Pexels.com https://www.pexels.com/photo/gardener-harvesting-apples-with-daughter-in-garden-5528990/?utm_content=attributionCopyText&utm_medium=referral&utm_source=pexels

Elijas, E. (2020). Person Pouring Water on Pickled Cucumber Jars [Online image]. Pexels.com https://www.pexels.com/photo/person-pouring-water-on-pickled-cucumber-jars-5503110/?utm_content=attributionCopyText&utm_medium=referral&utm_source=pexels

Green, V. (2020). [Untitled online image of dandelions]. Unsplash. https://unsplash.com/photos/i-uBAOo_BBA

Kemper, J. (2021). [Untitled online image of rhubarb plant]. Unsplash. https://unsplash.com/photos/1HHrdIoLFpU

Klein, D. (2016). Fresh Tomato Sauce [Online image]. Unsplash. https://unsplash.com/photos/FzB_512zvP0

K, P. (2019). [Untitled online image of a slice of berry cake]. Unsplash. https://unsplash.com/photos/Em-w4Kctk0Y

May, C. (2020). Glass of cocktail with lemon [Online image]. Pexels.com https://www.pexels.com/photo/glass-of-cocktail-with-lemon-5947101/?utm_content=attributionCopyText&utm_medium=referral&utm_source=pexels

Medina, F. (2019). [Untitled online image of a fire in a pan]. Unsplash. https://unsplash.com/photos/Uty8TYnGA44

Melnyczuk, T. (2021). [Untitled online image of lemon marmalade]. Unsplash. https://unsplash.com/photos/RUqnlEBa_7g

Olsson, E. (2018). Meal Prep for Breakfast & Lunch [Online image] Unsplash. https://unsplash.com/photos/P4jRJYN33wE

Pflug, S. Hand Holding Freshly Canned Salsa Photo [Online image]. Burst. https://burst.shopify.com/photos/hand-holding-freshly-canned-salsa?c=harvest

Pixabay. (2016). Clear Glass Mason Jars [Online image]. Pexels.com https://www.pexels.com/photo/clear-glass-mason-jars-48817/?utm_content=attributionCopyText&utm_medium=referral&utm_source=pexels

Primeau, N. (2019). [Untitled online image of measuring spoons]. Unsplash. https://unsplash.com/photos/mcbSkZ3l0xc

Rai, A. (2020). Fresh off the vines [Online image]. Unsplash. https://unsplash.com/photos/6P36fWsCypU

RODNAE Productions. (2020). A Person Putting a Jam on a Bread [Online image]. Pexels. https://www.pexels.com/photo/a-person-putting-a-jam-on-a-bread-5848004/?utm_content=attributionCopyText&utm_medium=referral&utm_source=pexels

Rutkowski, A. (2016). Fresh strawberries [Online image]. Unsplash. https://unsplash.com/photos/GdTLaWamFHwSays, C. (2016, July 20)

www.ingramcontent.com/pod-product-compliance
Lightning Source LLC
Chambersburg PA
CBHW081708100526
44590CB00022B/3703